Ephraim George Squier

Collection of rare and original Documents and Relations

Concerning the Discovery and Conquest of America

Ephraim George Squier

Collection of rare and original Documents and Relations
Concerning the Discovery and Conquest of America

ISBN/EAN: 9783337176396

Printed in Europe, USA, Canada, Australia, Japan

Cover: Foto ©ninafisch / pixelio.de

More available books at **www.hansebooks.com**

COLLECTION

OF

RARE AND ORIGINAL

Documents and Relations,

CONCERNING

The Discovery and Conquest of America.

CHIEFLY FROM THE SPANISH ARCHIVES.

No.  *I.*

Published in the Original,

WITH TRANSLATIONS, ILLUSTRATIVE NOTES, MAPS, AND BIOGRAPHICAL SKETCHES,

BY E. G. SQUIER, M. A., F. S. A.

Member of the Society of Antiquaries of France; Royal Society of Antiquaries of Denmark; Archæological Institute of Great Britain; American Ethnological Society, &c., &c., &c.

ALBANY:

J. MUNSELL, 78 State Street.

MDCCCLX.

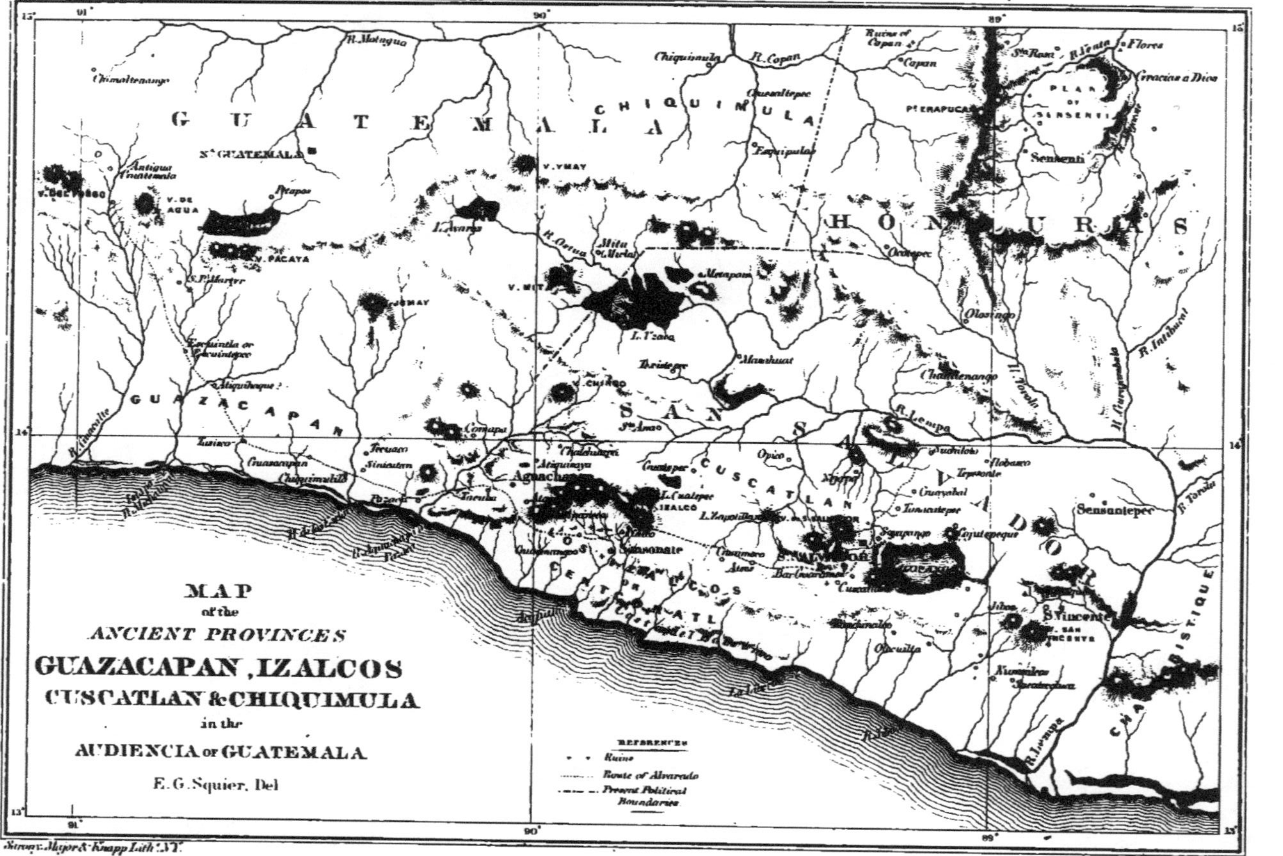

Strong, Major & Knapp Lith. N.Y.

CARTA

DIRIJIDA AL

REY DE ESPAÑA,

POR EL

Licenciado Dr. Don

DIEGO GARCIA DE PALACIO,

Oydor de la Real Audiencia de Guatemala;

Año 1576.

Being a Deſcription of the Ancient Provinces of Guazacapan, Izalco, Cuſcatlan, and Chiquimula, in the Audiencia of Guatemala:

WITH

An Account of the Languages, Cuſtoms and Religion of their Aboriginal Inhabitants, and a

DESCRIPTION OF THE RUINS OF COPAN.

PREFATORY NOTE.

THIS Relation of the Licentiate Dr. Don *Diego Garcia de Palacio,* Auditor of the Audiencia of Guatemala, written in 1576, and addreſſed to the King of Spain, is now for the firſt Time publiſhed in the original Spaniſh. It is from a manuſcript Copy made by the Hiſtorian *Muñoz,* and preſerved in the Royal Academy of Hiſtory at Madrid.[1] A French tranſlation was publiſhed at Paris in 1840, by *M. Ternaux-Compans,* in a Work entitled *Recueil de Documents et Mémoires Originaux ſur l'Hiſtoire des Poſſeſſions*

[1] Acknowledgment is due to BUCKINGHAM SMITH, Eſq., late Secretary of the Legation of the United States in Madrid, for procuring and verifying the Manuſcript from which the Spaniſh Text of this Relation is printed. The Publick is already largely indebted to his intelligent Zeal for the Publication of a moſt valuable Collection of original Documents, obtained from the Spaniſh Archives, entitled, *Colleccion de Documentos para la Hiſtoria de Florida, y Tierras Adyacentes,* as well as for previous Tranſlations of rare Tracts and Papers illuſtrative of the Hiſtory of Florida.

Efpagnoles dans l'Amérique, etc. But the Tranflation, in a number of important Refpects, is both imperfect and inaccurate, and fails, as all Tranflations muft fail, in meeting the Requirements of the critical Student. It is with a full Confcioufnefs of this inevitable Refult, that I prefent a Tranflation of my own; but I confider that the Prefumption of the Attempt is atoned for by the Circumftance, that I give, at the fame Time, the original Text, fo that every Inquirer may form his own Eftimate of its Senfe, and of the Spirit which pervades it. To me the Relation has a fpecial Intereft. I have been over a great Part of the Ground that was traverfed by its Author, and I am deeply impreffed with the Accuracy of his Defcriptions. Nothing could be more Exact than his Accounts of the phyfical Features and natural Productions of the Diftricts of Country which he vifited, and his Truthfulnefs, in thefe Refpects, infpires complete Confidence in thofe portions of his Narrative which we are no longer able to verify. He was a clofe Obferver, and a careful Narrator, and his Memoir to the King of Spain will always ftand as one of the beft Illuftrations of an interefting Country, as it was at

the Period immediately ſucceeding the Conqueſt. It ſeems that in Obedience to a general Order of the Crown, addreſſed to the Audiencias, Palacio was deputed to viſit a Number of the Provinces of Guatemala; but Circumſtances which he alludes to, in the cloſing Paragraphs of his Relation, limited his inquiries to that Part of the Coaſt of the Pacific, lying between the river *Michatoyat* on one ſide and the river *Lempa* on the other, and extending Inland as far as the Ruins of *Copan* and the City of *Chiquimula* — a Diſtrict one hundred and fifty Miles long by a hundred Miles broad, or rather leſs than a twelfth of the Area compriſed in the ancient Audiencia of Guatemala. The Memoir in Fact, relates principally and eſſentially to the ancient *Cuſcatlan*, the preſent Republick of San Salvador, which was found occupied by a People of the Nahuatl or Mexican Stock, ſurrounded on all ſides by Nations of different Languages, towards ſome of whom they held a Poſition of Superiority, and by ſome of whom they were regarded with Hoſtility and Contempt. No rational Account of their Origin, nor even a plauſible Tradition reſpecting it has reached us; and the Problem whether, in common with another Family of the

ſame Stock, on the Shores of Lake Nicaragua, they were a Colony from the Plains of Anahuac, and an offſhoot from the Mexican Empire, or conſtituted the parent Stock whence the latter Sprung — for the Preſent at leaſt, this Problem remains open to Inveſtigation, and without a ſatisfactory Solution.

The Relation of Palacio was largely uſed by *Herrera*, who drew from it the whole of Chapters viii, ix, and x, of the Eighth Book of his Fourth Decade. But his Extracts were careleſſly made, and in a few Inſtances convey a different Meaning from the Original. Nor were they in all Reſpects judicious, at leaſt as regards modern Requirements, ſince ſome of the moſt intereſting Portions are not only omitted, but passed over without Notice. The preſent Publication will ſupply theſe Omiſſions, and furniſh new and valuable Materials for Hiſtorical and Archæological Inquiry. As regards the general Character of the People of Cuſcatlan, but eſpecially as regards their religious Rites and Ceremonies, it is probably ſufficiently full and ſatisfactory. It does not treat of their civil and political Organizations, inaſmuch as theſe had diſappeared, or had been greatly modified under the Authority of the Spaniards. As regards the Coun-

try itſelf, and its more remarkable Features, Productions and Reſources, I repeat, it is equally Exact and Intereſting. But probably the moſt intereſting Part of the Relation, is the Account which it contains of the Ruins, ancient even when Palacio wrote, and now known, from their Proximity to the little Town of that Name, as the Ruins of Copan. The wonderful Accuracy of Palacio's Deſcription of theſe Remains will appear on comparing it with the Accounts of *Galindo* and *Stephens*, and the Drawings of *Catherwood.* The "Giants," with what he regarded as Armor "in Moſaic," and with "Ribbons around their Legs"; the "Biſhops" with "Rings on their Fingers" and holding "Packets, reſembling Boxes" in their Hands; the Altars, or ſacrificial Stones, with Grooves and Reſervoirs "for the Blood of the Victims"; the graduated Pyramids; the great Circus reſembling the "Coliſeum of Rome;" the Terrace dominating the River, with its flights of Steps reaching to the Water; the ſubterranean Paſſages — nothing could be more graphic or truthful than his Account of them all. And it is remarkable, not to ſay inexplicable, that Herrera ſhould have wholly omitted any Alluſion to theſe Monuments. None of the Conquerors

mention them, nor do they appear to have been noticed by any of the Chroniclers of the Country down to the Time of *Fuentes*, who wrote in 1689, upwards of one hundred Years after Palacio. From his Manufcript, *Juarros*, in 1809, drew a brief Notice of them, which is not however, either in Completenefs or Accuracy, at all comparable with that of Palacio. Later, in 1835, Col. Galindo, an Officer in the Service of the Republick of Central America, publifhed a fhort Defcription in the Tranfactions of the American Antiquarian Society, and in the Proceedings of the Geographical Society of Paris. And finally, in 1841, they were in good part defcribed by Stephens, and admirably illuftrated by Catherwood, and for the firft Time, fairly prefented to the World — a Wonder to the Curious, and an Enigma to the Student.

Galindo[2] who had an inquiring Mind, but a very fuperficial Education, mifled by the Name given

[2] The Words of Galindo are as follows: "Palenque was abandoned, and the Memory of its Exiftence appears to have been obliterated before the Conqueft; whereas the Spaniards found Copan inhabited and in the Summit of its Perfection. * * * * A fmall Spanifh Force with a confiderable Number of auxiliary Indians, defpatched from Guatemala, captured this Place, though they met with great Oppofition on their March, and a Refiftance here worthy of better Means and Succefs." (*Trans. Am. Antq. Soc.*, II, 549.)

to the Ruins, believed them to be the Remains of the Town of Copan, captured and deſtroyed by *Hernando de Chavez* in 1530. Stephens, alſo, fell into ſome Confuſion on the Subject, and copied out Juarros's Account of the Capture of Copan; yet the extent and evident Antiquity of the Monuments forced him to doubt the Identity of the Spot with that of the Town deſtroyed by Chavez. And although it is ſcarcely poſſible that any well-informed Student in American Archæology ever fell into the ſame Error with Galindo, yet whatever doubts may have exiſted on the Subject, and as regards the high Antiquity of the Ruins of Copan, or rather of the nameleſs Ruins near Copan, they are ſet at Reſt by this Account of Palacio. They were evidently very nearly in their preſent Condition, at the Time he wrote, three hundred Years ago, and within fifty Years of the Conqueſt. Even then their Hiſtory was unknown, and only the vagueſt Traditions exiſted regarding them. So far as theſe Traditions indicate that they were built by the ſame People who built Palenque and Uxmal, and who left maſſive Monuments of their Skill, all the Way from Nicaragua to Mexico, there can be no doubt of their accuracy. The Hiero-

glyphics, ſo called in want of a better Deſignation, found on the Altars and Monoliths of Copan, are Identical in Character with thoſe of Palenque, and with thoſe which have come down to us in ſome of the aboriginal Paintings. On the ſcore of Antiquity, it may be added, there are various Reaſons for believing, that both Copan and Quirigua antedate Oloſingo and Palenque, preciſely as the Latter antedate the Ruins of Quiché, Chichen-itza and Uxmal, and that all of them were the Work of the ſame People, or of Nations of the ſame Race, dating from a high Antiquity, and in Blood and Language preciſely the ſame that was found in Occupation of the Country by the Spaniards, and who ſtill conſtitute the great Bulk of its Population.

It is proper to ſay in Concluſion, and in Extenuation of any Obſcurities or Inaccuracies in the following Relation, that the Manuſcript from which it is printed is not always legible, is imperfectly punctuated, and moreover abounds in ancient Forms of Orthography and Expreſſion, which ſometimes leave the Tranſlator in doubt as to the Author's meaning, and defy the Ingenuity of the Compoſitor to make the Text intelligible. Thoſe

who are beſt acquainted with the early Spaniſh Manuſcripts, are also beſt acquainted with the Difficulties in the Way of making them out, and will be the moſt lenient in reſpect to any Blunders, into which the Editor and Tranſlator may have fallen.

New York, July, 1859.

BIOGRAPHICAL NOTE.

THE Author of the following Relation, Doctor Don DIEGO GARCIA DE PALACIO, was Auditor of the Royal Audiencia of Guatemala, and afterwards of that of Mexico. He ſeems to have been a Man of conſiderable Intelligence and Activity, with a ſtrong martial Tendency, as ſhown in his various Memoirs and Papers. Nothing is known of his Works anterior to that which is here preſented. In the ſame Year in which it is dated, we find his Name in a Contract made with one *Diego Lopez* of Truxillo in Honduras, for the Conqueſt and Colonization of the Province of Taguz-galpa, which Name was applied to the Atlantic Coaſt of Central America, between Cape Camaron and the River San Juan, including the whole of what is now called the Moſquito Shore. He acted on behalf of the Audiencia of Guatemala, under Authority of a royal Cedula dated from Madrid, 10th of February, 1576. This Conceſſion was concluded

December 4th of the ſame Year, and the Original is preſerved in Seville, Roll 12 of the Documents entitled *Buen gobierno de Indias.* In this he is entitled "El Iluſtre Señor Licenciado Diego Garcia de Palacio, Oydor de la Real Audiencia de Guatemala, etc."

On the 8th of March 1578, he addreſſed a Letter to the King of Spain on the Conqueſt and Pacification of the Philippine Iſlands, entitled, *Carta al Rey, ſobre la Conquiſta y Pacificacion de las iſlas Filipinas, y las Ventajas de hacerſe la Navigacion para ellos deſde el Puerto de Fonſeca.*

The Original exiſts in Seville, among the Papers entitled *Papeles tocantes á las Iſlas de Poniente,* for the Years 1570-1588. In this Palacio ſtrongly urged the change of the Tranſit between the Atlantic and Pacific, from Mexico and Panama, to the Route through Honduras from Puerto de Caballos to the Bay of Fonſeca.

Palacio aſpired to be Governor of the Philippines, and in the Letter referred to, offered to reduce thoſe Iſlands at his own Coſt, in caſe the Crown ſhould entruſt him with the Appointment; but the Application does not appear to have met with Favour.

On the 30th of April 1579, he addreſſed another Letter to the Crown, from the Port of Realejo in Nicaragua, giving an Account of the "Robberies made by the Corſair Francis Drake on the Coaſts of Peru," etc., which is alſo preſerved in Seville.

After reaching Mexico, Palacio publiſhed two Works in that City, of which the Titles are:

Dialogos Militares de la formacion é informacion de perſonas, inſtrumentos y coſas neceſſarias para el buen uſo de la guerra. — Méjico, Pedro Ocharte, año 1583. In 4to.

Inſtruccion náutica para el buen uſo y regimiento de las Naos, su traza y gobierno, conforme á la altura de Méjico. — Méjico, año 1587. In 4to.

The Latter was dedicated to Don Alvaro Manrique de Zuñiga, Marqués de Villamanrique, Viceroy and Captain General of New Spain. It is divided into four Books, treating of the Sphere, the Uſe of the Aſtrolabe, the Gregorian Reform of 1582, the Golden Numbers, and other Points of the Calendar, with Directions for general Navigation, a Dictionary of Maritime Phraſes, etc., etc.

In September 1587, Palacio was made Captain General of the Armada which was ſent out, in that Year, from Acapulco againſt the Engliſh Cor-

ſairs who then infeſted the South Sea. His Commiſſion, which is ſtill preſerved at Seville, among the Papers brought from Simancas, gives him great Latitude of Action "as one well verſed and practiſed in all Things connected with the Sea." The Reſult of his Expedition is not known, and with this Appointment, Palacio ſeems to have diſappeared from Hiſtory.

CARTA

DIRIJIDA AL

REY DE ESPAÑA,

POR EL

Licenciado Dr. Don

Diego Garcia de PALACIO,

Oydor de la Real Audiencia de Guatemala;

Año 1576.

C. R. M.—Por Vueſtras cédulas y proviſiones eſtá mandado i hordenado á los Virreyes, Preſidentes i Gobernadores deſtas partes, hagan larga i verdadera relacion de la poſicion de tierras, Indios, lenguas, coſtumbres, rios,

YOUR *R. C. Majeſty*, by divers decrees, has ordered that your Viceroys, Preſidents, and Governors in theſe parts ſhall give to you an exact and detailed deſcription of the geography of their various diſtricts, and of the mountains and rivers found in them, and of the languages and cus-

montes i variadades i cosas de sus districtos, de que deba darse quénta á V. M., i ponerse por memoria; asi se debe creher lo habrian fecho, y como cosa cumplida no trataré dello. Por otras ansi mismo manda V. M. que un Oydor por su turno ande visitando las provincias de su partido, para la buena conservacion é pulicia destos naturales i desagraviarlos de las injusticias i vexaciones que padescen i á componer i hacer justicia en las demas cosas que entre ellos se ofrecen. En cuyo cumplimiento esta V. R. Audiencia de Guatemala me nombró para la dicha visita, i señaló algunas provincias de su districto donde ví i averigué algunas cosas, que de raras i de consideracion me an forzado á dar quenta á V. M., aunque con rudo estilo.

Conocida cosa es que del ámbito del mundo, que segun la comun opinion es 5625 leguas, posehe i gobierna V. M. la mayor parte como consta por su posicion, porque, sin esos Vuestros Reynos de España, Italia, Flandes, ay á las Islas del Poniente, do Vuestros Ejercitos van ampliando V. R. Corona, 3405 leguas, regulados los paralelos i fecha la computacion á las comunes españolas, en que se incluye este districto, que comienza de los postreros terminos de Teguantepeque, i acaba en los de Costa-rica, corre S. E. y N. O. 300 i mas leguas. Está dividida en 13 provincias principales, sin otras mas menudas que en ellas se incluyen; son Chiapa, Soconusco, Suchitepeques, Cuauhthemalan, Vera-paz, Izalcos, San Salvador, San Miguel, Honduras,

toms of the Indians—in ſhort, an account of all the things deſerving to be mentioned. As I ſuppoſe that theſe orders have been executed, I ſhall not treat of all theſe matters. But Your Majeſty has alſo ordered, that each member of the Audiencia, in his turn, ſhall make a journey throughout its juriſdiction, to ſee to the conſervation and regulation of the natives, to defend them againſt vexations and injuſtice, and to arrange and ſettle equitably all difficulties which may ariſe among them. In compliance with theſe orders, Your Royal Audiencia of Guatemala having choſen me to undertake this duty, and having deſignated certain provinces within which to make my inquiries, I now proceed, although in a rude way, to give to Your Majeſty an account of the rare and curious things which fell under my notice.

It is a well known thing, that of the whole circumference of the earth, which according to received opinion is 5625 leagues, Your Majeſty poſſeſſes and governs the greater part; for from your kingdoms of Spain, Italy, and Flanders to the Iſlands of the Weſt, where your armies are engaged in extending your dominion, there are 3405 Spaniſh leagues, including this diſtrict, which commences at the lower extremity of Tehuantepec, and reaches, on the S. E., to Coſta Rica, and has a total length of upwards of 300 leagues. It is divided into 13 principal provinces, not enumerating a number of others leſs conſiderable, which are included in

Choluteca, Nicaragua, Taguz-galpa, Cofta-rica; i en cada una dellas ay i hablan los naturales diferentes lenguas, que pareze fue el artificio mas mañofo que el demonio tuvo en todas eftas partes para plantar difcordia, confundiendolos con tantas i tan diferentes lenguas como tienen, que fon:

En la de Chiapa, Chiapaneca, Tloque, Mexicana, Zozil, Zeldal-quelen.

En la de Soconufco, la Mejicana corrupta, i la materna, é Vebetlateca.

En la de los Suchitepeques i Cuahutemala, Mamey, Achi, Cuahtemalteca, Chienanteca, Hutateca, Chirichota.

Los Izalcos i Cofta de Guazacapan, la Popoluca, i Pipil.

La Verapaz, Poconchi, Caechicolchi.

La de Sn. Salvador, Pipil i Chontal.

El valle de Acacevaftlan i el de Chiquimula de la Sierra, Tlacacebaftleca y Apay.

En la de San Miguel, Poton, i Taulepa Ulua.

La Choluteca, Mangue, Chontal.

En Honduras, Ulba, Chontal, y Pipil.

Nicaragua, Pipil corrupto, Mangue, Maribio, Ponton, i Chontal.

En la de Taguz-galpa, la materna i Mexicana.

En la de Cofta-rica y Nicoya, la materna i Mangue.

De las quales comenzé a vifitar de la de Guazacapan hafta el rio de Lempa, que corre 50 leguas al Efte por la Cofta del Sur, i á lo hancho hafta

them, viz: Chiapa, Soconuſco, Suchitepeques, Cuauhthemalan,(1) Vera Paz, Izalcos, San Salvador, San Miguel, Honduras, Choluteca, Nicaragua, Taguz-galpa, and Coſta Rica.

The inhabitants, of each of theſe provinces, ſpeak different languages, which without doubt originated in an adroit device of the devil, in order the more eaſily to ſow the ſeeds of diſcord among them. (2) Theſe languages are:

In the province of Chiapa, the Chiapaneca, Tloque, Mexicana, Zozil, Zeldal-quelen.

In the province of Soconuſco, a corrupt Mexican, the Ubetlateca, and the mother language of the country.

In Suchitipeques and Cuahutemala, the Mamey, Achi, Cuahtemalteca, Chienanteca, Hutateca, and Chirichota.

Among the Izalcos, and on the coaſt of Guazacapan, the Popoluca and Pipil. (3)

In Vera Paz, the Poconchi, Caechicolchi.

In San Salvador, the Pipil and Chontal.

In the Valley of Acacevaſtlan, and in that of Chiquimula de la Sierra, the Tlacacebaſtleca and Apay.

In San Miguel, the Poton, Taulepa, and Ulua.

In Choluteca, the Mangue and Chontal.

In Honduras, the Ulba, Chontal, and Pipil.

In Nicaragua, a corrupt Pipil, the Mangue, Ponton, Marabio, and Chontal.

In the province of Taguz-galpa the mother language, and the Mexican.

Chiquimula de la Sierra, que corre 30 leguas Norte-Sur, en que viſite 156 lugares de Eſpañoles é Indios i entre ellos cuentanſe i repartí 78, de lo que los naturales deben pagar de tributo, en cada un año, á ſus encomenderos.

La dicha Coſta comienza deſde el Rio de Michiatoya i ſe fenece i acaba en el de Aguachapa. Es abundante de montes, aguas, cazas, i peſca de todas ſuertes; tiene mucho frutales de la tierra i de Caſtilla, boniſimas naranjas, i algunos higos, i melones. Es tierra de cacao, y de buenas tierras para mayz, y las demas legumbres i ſemillas que los Indios huſan; tiene comodidad toda ella para hacer ſal, aunque la hacen con mucho trabajo i rieſgo de ſu ſalud. Sacan la ſalmuera, que para hacella an meneſter de la tierra que la mar baña en ſus crecientes, i cuezenla en hornos ſemejantes á los que los campaneros huſan; gaſta mucha leña i ollas para cocerla por manera, que aunque ſe podria hacer mucha, es coſtoſa, enferma, i trabajoſa de hacer. Tiene muchos eſteros de que ſe aprovechan de grandes peſquerias de todo genero de peſcados i tortugas, aunque tienen i eſtán llenos de caymanes, que propiamente ſon los cocodrillos, porque tienen las eleciones que dellos qüentan los naturales; i eſpanta peſcar en ellos, porque alliende de la fiereza que mueſtran i grandeza que tienen, eſtán algunos muy encarnizados i cebados; i acontecido que paſando un gran toro por un rio le aſio uno de la cola, i hera tan grande que aunque ſalido

In that of Cofta Rica and Nicoya, the indigenous language and the Mangue.

Of thefe provinces, I traverfed firft that of Guazacapan, going as far as the river Lempa, which is 50 leagues to the Eaftward, following the South Coaft; and thence I went inland as far as Chiquimula de la Sierra, a diftance of 30 leagues from North to South; in which diftrict I vifited 156 villages of Spaniards and Indians, of which I enumerated and fet off 78 wherein the Indians fhould pay every year the amount of tribute affeffed on them to their *encomenderos*.

The faid Coaft of Guazacapan commences at the river Michatoyat, and terminates at that of Aguachapa. (4) It is abundantly wooded and watered, and contains every variety of fifh and game. It is very productive in fruits of the country and of Spain, and produces furthermore excellent oranges, figs, melons, and cacao. Maize grows well, as alfo all the grains and vegetables ufed by the Indians. There is every facility for making falt, although the Indians do not know how to manufacture it, except with great labor and at the rifk of their health. They take the brine made by the fun from the water left by the higheft tides, which they reduce in ovens fimilar to thofe which bell-founders ufe, at a coft of large quantities of wood and earthen pots. They might make more if they were acquainted with a better mode of reduction than this, which is difficult, coftly, and unhealthy.

el toro á la horilla, él tiró lo que pudo para desasirse i salir á tierra, no pudo porque el cayman hera tan grande i feroz que lo tornó al agua i mató! Otros estragos i daños han sido en diversas partes destas provincias que admira, aunque con toda su fiereza ay muchos Indios que se hechan al agua i chapuzados debajo le atan pies i manos i dan cabo á otros Indios que quedan en tierra i ansi los sacan fuera del agua i los matan. Llegando yo á un lugar, por me regalar me convidaron para que lo viese, no lo quise acceptar por el riesgo que parece ofrece la braveza de un animal tan espantoso, los quales i sin que yo lo supiese fueron i ataron uno como dicho es i me lo traxeron. Ay algunos dellos 20, 30 i mas pies, muy gruesos, de gruesos pies i manos, la cola gruesa i recia, hieren con ella bravisimamente. Tienen muchas conchas i que no las pasa un arcabuz, á veces la boca muy grande con dientes fierisimas repartidos en tres andánas; yo conté á un 34 dientes en cada una, sin los colmillos con que atrabiesa el ocico superior por dos agujeros que naturaleza le hizo. Tiene toda esta costa muchas praderias que acá llaman zabanas, grandes i de mucho pasto, i en ellas algunas estancias de vacas, aunque no las que podria haber segun su grandeza i grosedad.

Es tierra enferma por la mucha calor i humedad que en ella ay, de que se suelen causar grandes calenturas i otros males pestilenciales, mosquitos de quatro generos que de dia desasosiegan i enfadan,

There are many creeks on the coaſt, in which they have large eſtabliſhments for catching all kinds of fiſhes and turtles, notwithſtanding that they are full of alligators, or rather crocodiles, very ferocious, and greatly feared by the people. They relate that a large bull, in paſſing a river, was attacked by a cayman, which ſeized him by the tail with ſuch force, that notwithſtanding he reached the ſhore and did his utmoſt to ſhake off his enemy, he was drawn back into the water and killed. The caymans have committed many ravages in other parts of this province; yet it is wonderful, notwithſtanding their ferocity, that there are actually many Indians who dive beneath them, in the water, and attach cords to their legs, in ſuch manner that they are dragged to the ſhore and ſlain. On my arrival at one of the villages, the inhabitants propoſed to entertain me with a feat of this kind, but I would not conſent to their incurring the riſk of encountering ſo fearful an animal. They nevertheleſs went off without my knowledge, and brought me one thus ſecured. Some of the caymans are from twenty to thirty feet and upwards in length, with large bodies and big feet, and covered with ſcales through which a muſket ball cannot pierce. Their tails are very powerful and dangerous; and their mouths are large, with three rows of formidable teeth. I counted thirty-four teeth in each range, beſides the eye-teeth, which fit into holes in the upper jaw.

i de noche no dejan dormir muchas moſcas, i abiſpas de diverſos generos malas i venenoſas que en picando hazen roncha, i ſi las raſcan llagan. Yo vi que un mozo cayó de una picadura atordido i amortecido por mas eſpacio de dos horas. Ay alacranes i unos guſanos peludos que con cualquiera coſa que de ſu cuerpo toquen emponzoñan i á veces matan; i otros que llaman cientopies tan malos i tan venenoſos como los dichos; grandes culebras i vivoras maliſſimas, i otras ſabandijas peſtilenciales i muy dañoſas, de diferentes eſpecies, que eſpantan con los malos efectos que ellas i con ellas hacen. Ay unas que crian un cornecuelo en la cabeza, de que los malos huſan para ſus ſucias lujurias, de efecto eſtraño; i para lo meſmo ay unos eſcarabajos muy grandes los cuernos de los quales aun ſon peores i de mas mala operacion. Yo hablé á un ſacerdote á quien unos ſus toſcos amigos le hicieron las raeduras de una burla tan peſada que ni bañarſe, ni ungüento roſado, ni ſangrarſe le aprovecho por mas de 24 horas. Ay en eſta provincia abejas blancas, aunque pocas. Hacen la miel i cera muy blanca, no pican tan mal como los otras hordinarias.

Ay en toda eſta tierra un arbol comun que noſotros llamamos *ciruelos* i los Indios *cotes*, que perdiendo las hojas, ſin ella crian i produzen i dan ſu fructo, i deſpues de dada, hechan hoja i ſeparan muy freſcos i lozanos como lozaneandoſe del fructo i beneficio que an dado.

On this coaſt are many plains, called in the country *Savannahs*, with abundant paſturage. In theſe there are ſome cattle farms, but not as many as from the great ſize of theſe *Savannahs* might be expected.

The country is unhealthy, in conſequence of its heat and humidity, which cauſe fevers and other peſtilent maladies, and produces moſquitos of four kinds, which torment one all the day and prevent him from ſleeping at night. There are alſo many venomous flies, and bees the ſting of which makes bliſters, that become ſores on rubbing. I ſaw a boy who fainted and remained inſenſible for upwards of two hours, in conſequence of having been ſtung by one of theſe inſects. There are alſo ſcorpions, and a kind of hairy worm which poiſons all things it touches, and ſometimes cauſes death; and alſo centipedes, as bad and venemous as the creatures already named; large ſerpents, and dangerous vipers—in ſhort, all kinds of unclean and deadly inſects, enough to make one tremble who reflects on the evils which they occaſion or which may be occaſioned by them.

Some of theſe have a little horn on their heads, which evil-minded perſons uſe in their filthy debaucheries, and which has an extraordinary effect. There is alſo a ſpecies of very large *ſcarabæus* of which the horns have a greater and ſtill worſe effect. I knew a prieſt, whom ſome of his rude friends induced to ſwallow ſome of the ſcrapings

El dicho rio de Michiatoya, donde eſta provincia comienza, nace i es un deſaguadero de la laguna de Amatitan, quatro leguas de Guatemala, i para caer á la dicha provincia, hace un ſalto tan grande que un arcabuz parece no podria llegar debajo arriba, i una concavidad entre el agua i peña donde cae muy grande, de manera que ſe crian en el gran ſuma de papagayos de diferentes suertes, i tantos murcielagos que es maravilla, que ſon tan malos que ſe dan é topan una ternera la matan i deſangran; cuelganſe en la dicha cueva unos de otros, i hazen razimos i colgajos mayores que un ſombrero, i en algunas partes ſe an deſpoblado eſtancias de ganado por el mucho daño que hacian en las dichas terneras.

En un lugar de aquella provincia, que ſe llama Neſticpac, ay unos lagos que parecen ſalen de mineros de azufre de mala agua i hedionda; ſalen á ſus trillas pedazos del dicho azufre quajados i conjelados de la groſedad del agua, tan limpio i purificado como la mejor que viene de Alemaña; i el paſto que riega las vertientes deſta agua es tan bueno para los caballos i engordan tanto que de muy perdidos i flacos en pocas dias vuelvan en ſi i ſeparan muy hermoſos i gordos.

Los Indios deſta provincia ſon humildes i de buena condicion; corre entre ellos la lengua Mexicana, aunque la propia es Popoluca; en ſu gentilidad huſaban de los ritos i idolatrias, ſueños i ſuprecticiones que los Pipiles i Chontales ſus vecinos, de que trataré adelante; en los mas lugares

from theſe horns; and for more than twenty-four hours, neither baths, unguents, nor bleedings could ſtop the conſequences of the pleaſantry!

White bees are found in this province, but in ſmall numbers. Their honey and wax have an extraordinary whiteneſs, and their ſting is not as ſevere as that of the ordinary varieties.

Throughout the country there is a very common tree producing a fruit which we call plums, and the Indians *cotes* [*jocotes*]. It ſheds its leaves when the fruit appears; but when the latter matures and is gathered, it throws them out again, freſhly and luxuriantly, as if rejoicing over the harveſt and benefits which it has given.

The river Michatoyat, where this province commences, riſes in the lake of Amatitan, four leagues from Guatemala. In reaching this province it precipitates itſelf over a fall ſo high that its top cannot be reached by a muſket ball. (5) There is a kind of cavern between the ſheet of water and the rock, within which are found parrots of various kinds, and a marvellous number of bats, which attach themſelves one to the other, forming cluſters as big as a hat. They are very miſchievous, and if they find a calf in the fields will kill it, by ſucking its blood. On ſome farms in the neighborhood, it is impoſſible to raiſe cattle, becauſe the bats deſtroy all the calves.

In a place in that province which is called *Neſticpac*, there are ſome ſmall lakes which appear to

ſe conozen ſus ſeñores naturales, heran poco poderoſos, valia i mandaba entre ellos mas el que mas podia mas, i tenia mas hombres de guerra.

Eſtá repartida en ſeys partidos de clerigos; ſon medianamente inſtruydos en la dotrina Criſtiana; en la pulicia van tambien aprovechando aunque como jente nueva en nueſtra coſtumbres ſi ſe deſcuydan dellos ſalen a la pega de ſu gentilidad. Alli ſe me querello un Indió que un ſu alcalde ſin ſu pedimento habia procedido contra ſu mujer i caſtigadola por ocho adulterios, i forzadole á él que pagaſe la condenacion que por ellos le habia fecho, por manera que allende de ſu afrenta le llevaban ſu dinero; el caſo es que en tiempo de ſu infidelidad, hera coſtumbre que quando alguna muger eſtaba de parto, la comadre hazia confeſaſe i dixeſe todos los pecados, para que haviendolos confeſado pariese mejor, i quando habiendolo fecho la tal muger no paria, llamaban á ſu marido, i hacian le él confeſaſe las ſuyos; i ſe eſto no aprovechaba quitavanle al tal marido el *maxtli* i pañetes que traya calzados é poniales en las renes de la preñada, i ſi eſto no haprovechaba para que parieſe, la propria comadre ſacaba ſu ſangre i ſacrificabala aſperjando con ella los quatro vientos, haciendo algunas invocaciones i ceremonias. Sucedio que eſtando la muger del querellante de parto ſe confeſo, oyendela un alguazilejo que eſtaba eſcondido, dixo que habia cometido adulterio con los ocho referidos; i deſpues de ſana el dicho alguazil la acuſo ante el alcalde dellos

flow from mines of ſulphur. Their water is bad and fœtid. At their edges are found cryſtalized maſſes of ſulphur, purer than the beſt which comes from Germany. The paſtures irrigated by the water are ſo excellent for horſes that the thinneſt and moſt reduced rapidly recover their powers, and come out in a few days ſleek and fat.

The Indians of this province are ſubmiſſive and of a good nature. The Mexican language is current among them, although their proper tongue is the Popoluca. Before their converſion, they had the ſame rites and idolatry with the Pipiles and Chontales their neighbors, of whom we ſhall ſpeak further on, and like them believed in dreams and other ſuperſtitions. In moſt parts they recognize their native chiefs, who however were not very powerful; thoſe who were ſtrongeſt or had moſt warriors give law to the others. ([6])

They are now diſtributed among ſix orders of prieſts, and moderately inſtructed in the Chriſtian faith. They begin to be civilized, but as they are new to our cuſtoms, if they are neglected, they will ſoon fall back into their idolatry. While there one of the Indians complained to me that the Alcalde had proſecuted his wife for adultery, without his having complained of her, and that he had been obliged to pay the fine; in conſequence of which, and to avenge his injury, he had ſtolen the money of the Alcalde. This affair happened as follows:

dichos delitos, i por ellos la prendió caſtigo é penó. Eſtan aun ſiempre eſtos naturales en algunos hierros i ceremonias antiguas, placera à Dios que, con la diligencia que ſe pone, poco á poco vayan olvidanoſe de ſu perdicion antigua, i tomando el camino verdadero para ſalvarſe.

No tiene eſta provincia puerto, ſino uno que llaman de Eztapa, donde antiguamente el Adelantado Pedro de Alvarado hizo ciertos navios pequeños. An querido algunos decir que ſera comodo para que, ſi V. M. fuere ſerbido ſepaſe por eſtas provincias la contratacion del Peru, ſe correſponda en el; es impoſible por muchas razones; ſu entrada es playa de mucho tumbo, deſabrigada i de mala facion para puerto; hace la mar una barra en la tierra arto grande i onda, mas en la entrada i boca muy baja, porque quando es mar muerto aun no ay un eſtado de agua, i por la bracuz ay reſaca i tumbo dicho la dicha boca ſe muda cada año adonde la fuerza de los tiempos hiérc mas recio. Dicen algunos, que para que la barra no ſe mude ſe podria hacer un muelle, que la fuerze ſiempre á eſtar en un lugar i no mudarſe; parece razon de poca conſideracion, para que allende que aunque eſtubiera ſiempre en un lugar i no mudarſe, es baxa i de poca agua, deſabrigada i que con los tiempos tiene mas ó menos arena por falta de cimiento que no tiene por ſer harena grueſa i lavada. No tiene V. M. hacienda en eſtas provincios para podello hacer en 20 años. Dizen tambien que en la dicha barra ſe podria

During their idolatry, the women, at the time of their accouchment, confeſſed all their ſins to the midwife; they believed that this facilitated parturition; but if notwithſtanding, the birth was difficult, the huſband was alſo obliged to confeſs his ſins; and if this did not anſwer, they took the breech-cloth (*maxtli*) or drawers of the huſband and placed them under her loins; and if this did not ſucceed, the midwife, as a laſt reſource, drew blood from her own perſon, and ſprinkled it to the four points of the compaſs, with ceremonies and invocations. The wife of the Indian in queſtion, at the time of her accouchment, confeſſed to the midwife that ſhe had eight lovers, whom ſhe named. This was heard by a concealed alguazil, who when ſhe became well, denounced her to the Alcalde, who in turn chaſtiſed her. (7)

Theſe Indians preſerve many of the errors and ceremonies of their ancient idolatry, but it is to be hoped that through the will of God, and by the diligence of his ſervants, they may be diverted, little by little, from their road to perdition, and led to take the true path to ſalvation.

There is but a ſingle port in this province called Eſtapa [Iſtapa], where in former times the Adelantado Pedro de Alvarado conſtructed ſome little veſſels. Certain perſons have alledged that it would be advantageous for Your Majeſty to make the route to Peru paſs through theſe provinces; but this is entirely impoſſible, ſince it is only an open road-

echar un rio que con ſu corriente haga mayor barra i boca i mas ondo, i mejor puerto; tampoco es bien conſiderado, porque allende que ſera muy coſtoſa i poco firme ſegun lo que la mar y remarſo haze entra en la tierra adentro, aunque en ella ſe hechaſen muchos rios, no havia ni podria hacer fuerza que contra la furia hordinaria de la mar i grande tumbo que ſiempre alli tiene, haga barra ni puerto conveniente; i quando contra ella obiera tanta agua i corriente que lo pudiera hacer la propia corriente, impidiera i eſtorbara que fuera puerto como quieren en decir que podria.

LA PROVINCIA DE LOS IZALCOS.

Que la coſa mas rica i grueſa que V. M. tiene en eſtas partes, comienza del rio Aguachapa i acaba en Guaymoco i Coſta de Tonala, corre por la meſma coſta 18 leguas. Tiene las calidades del ſuelo i cielo que la de Guazacapan, i abundancia de cacao, peſca, i frutos, i demas coſas que acá comunamente ay en las tierras calientes, i en eſpecial la mas abundante de cacao que ſe ſabe. El arbol.que da el cacao es mediano, tiene ſus hojas como caſtañal, aunque mayores; produze flor i fruta caſi todas las lunas, i lo meſmo hacen en eſtas partes todas los naranjos. Echa ſu flor el tronco i ramas, comenzando las mas veces deſde el ſuelo, i como ellos echan la flor i crian ſu fructo, de que ſe van criando unas mazorcas mas largas i mayores que piñas; i dentro dellas 25 ó 30 almendras, que

ſtead, incommodious and without ſhelter. The ſea has made ſo bad a bar at its mouth that it is difficult to go into it at low tide, and the ſtorms change the entrance every year. There are thoſe who pretend, that to prevent this bar from conſtantly changing its place, it is only neceſſary to conſtruct a mole which will keep it fixed; but even then the port would only be a little leſs bad than now—ſhallow, without ſhelter, and filling up conſtantly, as it appears that the bottom of the ſea is only coarſe ſand and pebbles, without coheſion. Beſides, this province does not afford the means of conſtructing a work of the kind propoſed, in twenty years. They pretend alſo, that a river may be turned to flow into the port, and thus deepen it, and cut through the bar; but they do not conſider the coſt of the undertaking, nor the difficulties interpoſed by the ſurf and the tides. ([8])

PROVINCE OF IZALCOS.

This is the largeſt and richeſt province which Your Majeſty poſſeſſes in theſe parts; it commences at the river Aguachapa and ends at Guaymoco, on the coaſt of Tonola, extending a diſtance of eighteen leagues along the ſea. It has the ſame qualities of ſoil and ſky with that of Guazacapan; is abundant in cacao, fruits, fiſh, and the other things which are generally found in hot countries; but in eſpecial, it is more abundant in cacao than any country known. The tree which produces

es el cacao, de las quales 200 valen comunamente entre los Indios un real; i es la moneda que, para las cosas menudos, corre de hordinario entre ellos i nosotros. Es tan tierno arbol que con qualquiera estremo se pierde i seca; i ansi para criarle es menester mucho cuydado, i ponelle otro arbol que llaman *madre*, que le haga sombra i hampare del sol i del ayre. Antiguamente hera tan estimado que nadie bebia del dicho cacao, que no fuese Caçique, gran Señor, ó valiente soldado. Usaban en el sembrallo muchas ceremonias; escojiendo de cada mazorca é piña los mejores granos de cacao i juntos lo que habrian menester, los zaumavan i ponian al sereno en quatro dias del pleni lunio, i quando los habian de sembrar se juntaban con sus mujeres con otras ceremonias bien sucias. En efecto hera la cosa mas preciada que acá habia; a crecido i multiplicadose tanto, despues que estan en Vuestra Real Corona, con la libertad que tienen devello i tratallo, que desta provincia principalmente i de su comarca se provee la Nueva España, de que ay mucho comercio i contratacion de una á otra parte. La calidad desta fructa es casi fria, en tercero grado; usase en las bebidas generalmente i gastase i cóxese tanto, que pareze que lo que sale á Nueva España i dan i gastan en sus casas i labores, debe ser, en solos quartro lugares de los Izalcos, mas que 50 mill cargas, que, á un precio comun, valen quinientos mill pesos de oro de minas. Yo los contó i repartí el tributo. Ocupan todos ellos, con sus huertas dos leguas

the cacao is of medium height; its leaf is like that of the cheſtnut but larger; and, like the orange trees of the country, it gives out flowers and fruit with almoſt every moon. The flowers ſtart indifferently from the ſtem and branches, all the way from the ground up, and when theſe fall the fruit makes its appearance. It is as large or larger than a pineapple, and contains from twenty-five to thirty ſeeds like almonds, which are the cacao beans, and of theſe 200 are of the value, among the Indians generally, of one rial. They ſerve for ſmall money or change, both among the Indians and the Spaniards. (9)

The cacao tree is very delicate, and suffers alike from too much heat and too much cold, and therefore requires a great deal of care. They plant at its ſide, in order to give it ſhade, and protect it from the winds, another tree, which is called its *Mother*. The beverage which they prepare from the cacao was formerly ſo highly eſteemed by the Indians, that no one was permitted to drink of it, unleſs he were a great perſonage, a cazique, or a famous warrior. In planting it, they uſed many ceremonies. They ſelected the beſt grains, and expoſed them for four nights to the full moon, and at the moment of planting them, the men had connection with their wives, and went through other ceremonies of a libidinous character. In ſhort, the cacao is the moſt precious thing produced here, and its cultivation has ſo much in-

en quadro, de que ſe infiere, no ſe ſaben tales leguas de arboles i huertas que fructifiquen, i den tanto valor. Quentan eſtos naturales el cacao por *contles*, *xiquipiles*, i cargas; un *contle* es 400 almendras, un *xiquipil* 20 *contles*, que ſon 8000 almendras; i una carga, 3 *xiquipiles*, con 24,000 almendras. Por eſtos numeros quentan todas las coſas, i es el mayor que entre ellos ſe halla. Pareció haber en la quenta de los dichos lugares * * * * vecinos i que todos tienen * * * * pies de los dichos cacaos.

En los terminos i coſta deſtos Izalcos, eſtá el puerto de Acajutla, donde ſurgen i eſtan los navios que andan al tracto del dicho cacao é mercaderias que vienen del Peru i Nueva Eſpaña.

Tambien ha querido decir que es bueno i ſuficiente para la correſpondencia á Peru, ſi V. M. fueſe ſervido que la que agora ay en Tierra Firme ſe paſaſe á eſta provincia. Eſtá en altura de 13 grados i 36 minutos, é por la diferencia del Meridiano de Sevilla al deſta tierra i declinacion ſe le da 4 minutos, con que ſeran 13 grados i 40 minutos. Corre leſte-hueſte i eſtá deſabrigado del ſur i ſus colaterales. Es una playa de mucha reſaca i tumbo, i no tiene facion ni talle de puerto, de mala i enferma poſicion, ſuſtentarſe los navios que alli ſurjen con todos los daños dichos, porque haze la mar en una recife que ay en la dicha playa una vuelta i reſaca de mar tan fuerte que hace eſtar los navios ſuſpenſos ſin hazer fuerza en los cables i ancoras; i eſte ſolo beneficio tiene para tantos daños i la ne-

creafed fince the country came under Your Royal Crown, in confequence of the liberty which now exifts for traffic in it, that this province and its neighborhood furnifh the principal fupply for all New Spain, with which there is much commerce, and where it is generally ufed, to fuch an extent indeed, that it is eftimated, that from but four villages of the Izalcos, there are exported upwards of 50,000 loads, valued, at ordinary prices, at 500,000 dollars. The quality of this fruit is cold, in about the third degree. ([10])

I made an enumeration of thefe Indians and affeffed their tribute. They occupy, with their gardens, two leagues fquare, and I known of no equal extent of land which has trees and gardens fo flourifhing, or which yields fo great value.

Thefe Indians count their cacao by *contles*, *xiquipiles*, and *cargas* or loads; one *contle* is 400 grains; the *xiquipil* is 20 *contles* or 8000 grains; and a *carga* is three *xiquipiles* or 24,000 grains. In this way they count all things, and it is the beft mode they have. It appears, in the enumeration of thefe villages, that there are * * * * inhabitants, each of whom has * * * * feet of ground for the cultivation of the cacao.

On the coaft and confines of thefe Izalcos, is the port of Acajutla, where veffels come to exchange the merchandife and products of Peru and New Spain for cacao. There are fome who pretend that this would be a good and adequate port

cesidad precisa que del tienen i falto de otro tal, é toda esta comarca i la comodidad i cercania que en el allan los vecinos i mercaderes de la villa de la Trinidad que esta poblada en los dichos Izalcos.

Estan situados en la falda de un volcan que está humeando, que segun todos afirman se ha consumido i ha bajado de 50 años á esta parte mas de 20 estados de altura; i algunos años arrojado i espedido de si tanta zeniza que a cubierto la tierra muchas leguas al rededor, y fecho gran daño en las huertas del cacao. Vierte la parte del Sur, como mas baja, muchas aguas, algunas muy buenas i otras malissimas i hediondas. Haze un rio que llaman de la Zeniza, por el mucho i gran hedor que lleba. Sale ansimismo del, otro arroyo de tan mala i viscosa agua que en poco tiempo cubre i haze piedra qualquiera cosa que en el cae. Y aconteció que habiendosele caydo á un Indio un machéte, al cabo de dos años se halló cubierto de mas de un palmo de piedra por todas partes. Y fuera destos Izalcos, en un lugar que se llama Tecpa, sale del dicho volcan otro arroyo de la mesma calidad. Dizen que en la provincia de Chiapa ay un rio que haze lo mesmo; i sacando unos Indios piedra, para hazer cal, i quebrando una halláron dentro un fuste de una silla gineta, sano i entero.

De los dichos Izalcos se van subiendo tres leguas hasta un lugar que se llama Apaneca, tan fresco i aun frio que es el estremo de los lugares dichos; cojense en el granadas, membrillos, manzanas, i

for the communication with Peru, if Your Majeſty were diſpoſed to change the tranſit from Tierra-firme to this province. It is in 13° 36′ of Latitude, or rather in 13° 40′, adding 4′ for the difference of the meridian of Seville. This roadſtead opens eaſt and weſt; it is unſheltered, with much ſurf, and has neither the form nor appearance of a port; it has a bad and unhealthy poſition; and the ſhips that viſit it are ſubjected to all kinds of danger, since the ſea breaks on a reef which there is here, with ſuch force, and makes ſuch a recoil, that they can only be held by the ſtrongeſt anchors and cables; hence they do not come here, except from neceſſity, for want of any other port, and from the importance of the trade of this diſtrict, and of the city of La Trinidad, which has been founded in this province. ([11])

This city is ſituated at the foot of a Volcano which ſmokes continually, and which I am aſſured has conſumed itſelf and diminiſhed in height more than twenty *eſtados* within fifty years. It has thrown out ſuch a quantity of cinders, at different times, as to cover the earth for many leagues around, doing great damage to the plantations of cacao. Falling from its ſouthern declivity, as well as lower down, are many ſtreams of water. In ſome of theſe ſtreams the water is excellent, in others bad and ſtinking. They form a river which is called *la Ceniza* (of the Aſhes), which emits a great ſtench. There is alſo another ſtream of ſuch

duraznos, trigo i las demas cofas que a eftas partes an venido defos Vueftros Reynos.

En el mefmo alto, una legua del, eftá otro que fe llama Ataco, del mefmo temple ifertilidad, i muy abundante de toda monteria i caza, por los muchos i buenos montes que para ella tienen. Tube noticia que habia en él venados de la forma que son los que en la India de Portugal crian la piedra bezar, é hife matar algunos en que fe hallaron algunas piedras, que probadas en enfermidades peftilentes hacen el mefmo efecto que las que fe traen de la dicha India. Ay tambien, un genero de ofos pequeños; no tienen boca, como los defos Reynos; tienen en el cabo del ocico un agujero pequeño i redondo, i para mantenerfe proveyólos naturaleza de una lengua larga, acanalada, con que chupan i facan la miel do quiera que la allan. I quando efta les falta, fe van á los hormigueros, donde tienden fu lengua como por caño y agujero de otra cofa engañandas las ormigas que entran i fe hartan dellas.

Ay afimifmo, muchas dantas de color blanco, pardo i vermejo, i otros muchos generos de animalejos eftraños i dañofos, i muchas ierbas i arboles de buenos efectos para la falud humana, almazigos, dragos, é arboles de ánime en mucha cantidad.

Profiguiendo en la vifita defte lugar, i pédiendo razon de los menores i huerfanos, para faber del tracto de fus perfonas i haciendas. Me traxeron una niña de año i medio, huerfana de padre i ma-

bad and viſcous water, that it covers with ſtone, or converts into ſtone, whatever article may fall into it. They relate that an Indian, who loſt his *machetė* in this ſtream, found it, at the end of two years, covered with a coating of ſtone more than a palm in thickneſs.

Beyond the diſtrict of Izalco, near a village called Tecpa, is found another ſtream flowing from this volcano, which has the ſame qualities. They ſay that there is a ſimilar one in the Province of Chiapa, from which ſome Indians took a ſtone, within which, on breaking it, they found the tree of a ſaddle, ſound and entire. ([12])

Leaving Izalco, and aſcending three leagues, we reach a place called Apaneca, which is freſh and cool, therein differing greatly from the villages already deſcribed. Here they cultivate pomegranates, quinces, apples, peaches, wheat, and, in one word, all the products of Spain which have been brought to theſe countries.

On the ſame elevated grounds, one league diſtant, is another village called Ataco, which has the ſame climate and products. Here are large and fine foreſts, affording good hunting and an abundance of game. I underſtand that the ſame kind of deer is found here, which, in the Portugueſe Eaſt Indies, furniſhes the bezoar ſtone, and that ſeveral have been killed, in which ſtones were found producing the ſame effect on peſtilential maladies. Here is alſo found a ſpecies of very ſmall bears

dre, que eſtaba en poder i la daba leche una vieja de mas de 70 años. I yo admirado que muger de tanta edad tubieſe leche, la hize traer delante de me, é vi como la niña la mamada averigue allende que hera dicha edad, que jamas habia parido ſino que al tiempo que tomo la dicha niña mobida de piedad i con animo de crialla, i porque no tenia quien la dieſe leche ſuficiente, la dio el pecho i le vino leche. Hizelo tomar por teſtimonio, i quiſe dieſe á entender á los Indios como por la caridad que aquella mujer habia tenido, Dios habio ſido ſervido huſar aquella maravilla contra la orden comun, para que los Indios ſe movieſen á miſericordia que lo han bien meneſter.

Del dicho lugar fuy á otro de Vueſtra Real Corona que ſe llama Aguachapa, de mediano temple, de la fertilidad i cazas dichas. Haceſe en él la mejor i mas galana loza al modo de los Indios, que ay en eſtas provincias Principalmente la hacen i es oficio de las mugeres, las quales labran ſin rueda ni inſtrumento alguno, mas que preparado el barro con las manos lo adelgazan, é ygualan de manera que hacen muy bien qualquier vaſija que les mandan. Ay en los terminos deſte lugar dos arroyos, i en el uno hacen los Indios pozos i remanſos de agua, en que ſe cria una nata i eſcrimento, que beneficiado ſe hace colorado como grana, i deſta hacen i dan color á unos jarros que hacen muy curioſos. Creo que es el bol armenico, porque tienen las eleciones del, i anſimeſmo lo ha dicho un me-

[ant-eaters], which inſtead of a mouth, has a ſmall round orifice at the extremity of the muzzle. Nature, to enable it to live, has given to this animal a long and hollow tongue, by means of which it ſucks up all the honey it can find. In lack of this, it thruſts its tongue into neſts of ants, and when the latter, miſtaking it for a tube or opening of ſome ſort, enter into it, the animal withdraws its tongue and ſwallows them.

There are alſo many white, fawn-colored, and ruſſet tapirs, and other ſtrange and noxious animals. Alſo many trees and plants of medicinal qualities, ſuch as maſtic, dragon's blood, and copal.

In viſiting this place, I took information related to minors and orphans, to know if they were protected in their perſons and property. They brought me a little girl, a year and a half old, who had loſt both father and mother, and who had been taken in charge and ſucked by an old woman, ſeventy years of age. Aſtoniſhed at this report, and that a woman of ſuch age ſhould give milk, I had her called before me and witneſſed the ſuckling of the child, with my own eyes. This woman had never borne a child, yet taking pity on the infant, who had nobody to give it ſuck, ſhe preſented her own breaſts, and the milk came. I had the teſtimony in the caſe taken down, and ſought to impreſs the Indians with the idea that this was a miracle, wrought by God himſelf, in recognition of the charity of the old woman.

dico, bebido aprobecha al flujo de ſangre y ace probado en enfermedades peſtilentes, y ha aprobechado mucho, debeſe creer que ſi lo es el agua do eſto ſe queja paſa por algun minero del dicho bol armenico. En el otro arroyo, con la meſma horden, coxen otra tierra negra con que dan muy buen color negro, aunque labado bacia. Ay en el termino del dicho lugar unos manantiales que yo ví de agua caliente i tanto que quema, i tan diferentes en el color i nacimientos que eſpantan. Llamanlo los Indios *el Infierno*, i no ſin alguna ſemejanza. Brotá i ſalé el agua en eſpacio de un tiro de balleſta, por muchas partes i con diverſos eſtruendos, ſegun los horganos por do ſalen; unos azen ruydo como ſuele un batan, otros como molino, otros como fuelles, otros como quien ronca, i de otras mil formas. En algunas partes ſale el agua turbia, en otras clara, en otras colorada, en otras amarilla i de otros colores, ſegun los mineros de tierra por do paſen, i del humo de allí ſale. Se haze un betun de diferentes colores que parece podria ſervir para pintar. Los Indios ſuelen llevar ſus hollas de *cotes* i de carne y cozellas en algun reſpiradero de aquella agua. Habra tres años que paſando un muchacho en el dicho lugar ſe le ſumió i undió una pierna en un pantano deſta agua, i aunque lo ſocorrieron luego, dejó la carne de toda la pierna, i ſacó el hueſo i nierbos mondos i limpios, i murió otro dia ſiguiente deſpues. De todas eſtas fuentes ſe haza un rio, que llaman el rio Caliente, que aunque ſale por

I went from here to another village called Aguachapa, which enjoys a medium temperature, and where are found the ſame products and the ſame kind of game. Here is made the beſt pottery, after the Indian manner, in all theſe provinces. It is chiefly manufactured by the women, without the aid of a wheel or other inſtrument, with their hands alone, in the uſe of which they are ſo dexterous as to give to their veſſels whatever ſhape may be deſired.

There are two ravines in the lands belonging to this village, in one of which the Indians open pits or reſervoirs for the water, whereon collects a kind of cream or ſcum, which, when prepared, gives as fine a color as cochineal. With this they paint their pottery in a very curious manner. I believe it to be *bole of Armenia*, for it has the ſame peculiarities; and a doctor aſſured me that when taken inwardly it cured the bloody flux, and that it has proved to be uſeful in peſtilential maladies. If this be ſo, we may believe that the water which flows in this ravine, traverſes a mine of *bole of Armenia*. In the other ravine, in the ſame manner, they obtain a kind of black earth, which gives an excellent black color; it however, waſhes out. Near this place I alſo found ſome ſprings of boiling water; they are of different origins and of various colors. The Indians call the place where they are found *Hell*, and not without ſome reaſon. They are all within the ſpace of a gun ſhot acroſs, and each

debajo de la tierra, mas de media legua defte lugar a contecido pelar los pies á un caballo i mancalle. Dos tiros de arcabuz mas cerca de una fierra que alli eftà, ay otros refpiraderos de agua caliente, i eftá una piedra de cinco varas de largo i tres de ancho, endida por medio, i fale fiempre por la endedura cantidades de humo; i llegandofe á ella fe oyé el mas orrible i efpantofo ruido que fe fale; y aconteсé muchas beces quando los tiempos andan rebueltos, que falen por alli unos bramidos i truenos que fe oyen media legua al derredor. Cofa por cierta que admira en el monte donde efto eftá, ay grandes i gruefos arboles, i un genero de robles de grandifimas bellotas de que los muchachos hazen tinteros; é yo tengo una concha de las dichas bellotas, que tienen tres dedos de gruefo. Ay en los terminos defte lugar efcorpiones tan grandes como gazapos, é un genero de fapos menores que ranas, que faltan por los arboles, i fe tienen como pajaros. En tiempo de aguas hazen tan grande eftruendo i dan tan grandes bramidos como unos terneros, i aunque efto me le habian afirmado no lo quife creher hafta vello; i anfimefmo las mayores ormigas que he vifto. Comenlas los naturales, i las venden en fus mercados.

Toda efta provincia efta repartida en 8 partidos de clerigos; i por el mucho comercio que en ella ay, es gente entendida é ladina, é inftruida por la mayor parte en las cofas de la Fee.

La provincia de Çençonatl fe acaba en el lugar

makes a different noiſe. One imitates a fuller's mill, another the ſound of a forge, and a third a man ſnoring; in fact they give forth a thouſand different noiſes. The water in ſome is clear, in ſome turbid, and in others red, yellow, and of various colors, according to the nature of the minerals which they contain, or of the ſmoke which riſes from them. They all leave depoſits of various colors, which it ſeems to me might be uſed for painting. The Indians are accuſtomed to place their veſſels over ſome of theſe openings, and thus cook their food. Three years ago, a boy paſſing here, one of his legs broke through the cruſt which had been formed over one of theſe ſprings, and although the limb was immediately withdrawn, it was deprived of its fleſh, and only the bones and tendons remained. The boy died on the ſecond day after. Collectively, theſe ſprings form a river called *Rio Caliente* (Hot River), which does not emerge from the earth for more than half a league from them, and even there is ſo hot as to burn the feet of horſes and make them lame. Double the range of a muſket ſhot from theſe ſprings, nearer a mountain which is found here, are other *reſpiraderos* of hot water. One of theſe is in a rock five yards long and three broad, which is ſplit in the middle, and from this opening it conſtantly ſends out ſmoke ([13]); and on approaching it, one hears a fearful ſound, which it is ſaid, at certain times, ſuch as the changes of the ſeaſons, reſembles thun-

dicho, i comienza la de Sn. Salvador en el de Atiquizaya, que es un lugarejo de V. R. Corona. Tiene las cazas é fertilidad dicho, tienen i hacen una masa i betun que llaman *axin*, de un género de gusanos ediondos i ponzoñosos, que is marabilloso medicamento para todo genero de frialdades y otras indisposiciones. Nace dos leguas deste lugar el rio que llaman de Aguachapa, y á 7 de su nacimiento va muy grande, i á 13, que es donde entra en el mar del sur, grandisimo. Creo que en todas las Indias no ay rio tan grande, con tan poca corriente.

De allí fuy al lugar de Sta. Ana; no tiene cosa de notar mas que de dos generos de madera, de las astillas de la una hacen i tienen la color leonada, i el otro palo si lo echan en el agua se torna azul. Estremadamente cerca del dicho está un lugarejo que se llama Coatan, i en sus terminos una laguna en la falda del volcan dicho, ondisima i de mala agua i muy llena de caymanes. Tienen dos isletas en medio. Los Indios Pipiles tenian esta laguna por un oráculo de suma autoridad, é que ningun humano podrá ver lo que en ella habia, i que el que probase se habia de tullir i morir mala muerte; i deribavan esta devocion de patrañas antiguas; en este herror mande que me hiciesen unas balsas para entrar en la dicha isla i desengañarles de tal torpeza. Estando fechas i para partirme pareze que ciertos negros i mulatos de una estancia alli vezina, entraron en la isla é hallaron un idolo grande de piedra de figura de muger, i algunos sacrificios.

der, and may be heard for a diſtance of half a league around. However this may be, one thing is certain and to be admired, and that is the foreſt in which this ſpring is found. The trees are tall and thick, and there is a kind of oak producing immenſe acorns, from which the boys make inkſtands. I have the ſhell of one of theſe, which is three inches in diameter.

There are hereabouts ſcorpions as large as young rabbits, and a kind of toad ſmaller than a frog, which mounts into the trees, and might be taken for a bird. In the rainy ſeaſon it makes a fearful noiſe, like that of a calf. Although I was told this, I could not believe it, until I ſaw the animal for myſelf. Here alſo, are found the largeſt ants that I ever ſaw. The natives eat them, and they are ſold in their markets.

This province is divided into eight eccleſiaſtical diſtricts; and in conſequence of its conſiderable commerce, its inhabitants are intelligent, ſagacious, and for the moſt part well inſtructed in the eſſentials of the Faith.

At the point laſt named, the province of Cençonatl terminates; that of San Salvador commences at Ataquizaya, a little village belonging to the crown. This has the ſame climate and productions with the towns juſt deſcribed; and here they make, from a ſtinking and venemous worm, a dough or paſte called *axin*, which is an admirable remedy againſt cold humors and other maladies.

Cerca hube de lo que ſe halló unos *Chalchibites* que ſon piedras de las que ſuelen aprobechar para la ijada orina é materias. Con lo qual los Indios viejos i antiguos ſe deſengañaron de ſu hierro, i los mozos mas Criſtianos entendieron la burla de aquel ſantuario ſer como las demas de ſu gentilidad.

Todos los lugares comarcanos ſon de buen temple é fertilidad, é de las demas buenas calidades dichas.

Con el término i montes del lugar Guaymoco de V. Real Corona, ay grandes arboles de balſamo, i en toda la coſta de Tonala, que es de ſu partido. En la igleſia del ví doce pilares del balſamo de á mas de 55 pies de alto. Es madera muy recia i peſada. El licor que en comun ſe coje del es por el bueno en el verano que acá es deſde Noviembre haſta Mayo; vale una botija peruléra del, doſcientos i quarenta reales. Los Indios ſácanlo con alguna violencia, porque para que el arbol dé é deſtile mas, lo chamuſcan con leña al derrido del tronco; yo he hecho ſacarlo i cojello como el arbol la da i deſpide, ſin otra fuerza de fuego ni inſtrumento. Dizen es licor marabilloſo; i que ſerá de mejor efecto hecha ſu ſemilla como almendras, i en ellas cria un licor como oro, hize ſacar un poco, tambien ſe cree que marabilloſa coſa; en abiendo ocaſion ſe eſparimentará, tambien hize ſacar de las meſmas pepitas agua, dicen las mugeres que es muy buena para agua de roſtro.

De alli ſe va á la ciudad de San Salvador por una

Two leagues from here the river Aguachapa takes its riſe; at a diſtance of ſeven leagues from its ſource it is a large ſtream, and at thirteen leagues, where it falls into the ſea, it is very large. I do not believe, that in all the Indies, there is ſo large a river with ſo ſhort a courſe.

From this place I went to Sta. Ana, where there is nothing remarkable except two kinds of wood, from the chippings of one of which, when ſoaked in water, is obtained a fawn color, and from thoſe of the other a fine blue. Very near here, is a little village called Coatan, in the neighborhood of which is a lake, ſituated on the flank of the volcano. (14) Its water is bad; it is deep, and full of caymans. In its middle there are two ſmall iſlands. The Indians regard this lake as an oracle of much authority. They believe that no man can endure to ſee what it contains, and that whoever makes the attempt will become dumb and die ſome fearful death. They derive this ſuperſtition from their ancient legends, and in view of it, I ordered ſome rafts to be made on the ſpot, to take me to the iſlands, in order to undeceive the Indians. They were made accordingly, but at the moment of embarking, I learned that certain negroes and mulattos of an adjacent eſtate had been there, and had found a great idol of ſtone, in the form of a woman, and ſome objects which had been offered in ſacrifice. Near by were found ſome ſtones called *chalchibites*, which are good againſt diſeaſes of the liver and

angoſtura i callejon eſtraño; páſaſe yendo por él un rio 67 vezes. Eſtá á la falda de un volcan grande, i de mucha circumferencia por ſus faldas; no echa fuego, porque la materia que la cauſaba ſe debio de acabar en el tiempo que ardio, conſumió é hizó tan gran boca que boxa mas de media legua, i eſtá ondiſima; i antes de llegar á lo bajo haze dos eſtancias ó plazas á la forma que ſon los que ſe hazen en los hornos de cal; de lo mas ondo é ultimo ſale un humo ordinario, i de tan grande hedor que ha contecido llegándoſe un Eſpañol cerca deſmayarſe, y amortecerſe. Deſde lo ultimo é bajo aſta lo mas alto eſtá lleno de grandes cedros, pinos, i otros muchos generos de arboles i animales, i de quemazones del fuego que ſolia haber en él.

Tres leguas de ſu eſtremidad eſtá un lugar que ſe llama Nixapa, donde ay un pedazo de monte áſpero que llaman *malpays*, de piedra i de mucha tierra quemada i arrojada, muy tendida i de grandes pedazos; i auſi pone admiracion donde pudo venir, pues en todo lo que ay haſta el dicho volcan no parece ſeñal de lugar de aya habido fuego; ſino en dicho volcan parece que pues las piedras y tierra que alli ay es que manda, i no ay lugar do mas cerca pudieſe ſalir que el dicho volcan lo arrojó al tiempo que tenia fuego, como lo an fecho en eſtas provincias uno que ay en el valle deſte ciudad, que pocas años ha hecho de ſi grandes montones de fuego i piedra; i otro de Nicaragua que rebentó i

bladder. ([15]) This vifit undeceived the old Indians, and convinced them of their errors, at the fame time that it gave the younger and Chriftianized Indians to underftand, that the ideas connected with this fanctuary were as abfurd as the other notions of their paganifm.

All the villages in this vicinity are of good climate, furrounded by a fertile foil, and poffefs the various good qualities already mentioned. In the diftrict of the village of Guaymoco, and in the forefts which pertain to it, as alfo in all the coaft of Tonala, are found balfam trees of large fize. In the church of the village, I faw twelve pillars of balfam wood, which were at leaft 55 feet high. It is a hard and heavy wood. The beft balfam is collected between November and May, and a bottle of it is valued at 40 rials. The Indians obtain it from the trees with fome degree of violence; and in order to make them diftil rapidly they build fires around their trunks. They fay that this balm is a marvellous liquor; and in order to give it greater effect, they extract an oil from the nuts of the trees, which looks like gold; alfo, a kind of liquid, which the women aver is very good as a cofmetic. ([16])

Going from here to the city of San Salvador it is neceffary to pafs through a defile exceedingly narrow, and to crofs the ftream which flows through it fixty-feven times. ([17]) The city is fituated on the flank of a very high volcano, of

ſubertió unas ſierras ſobre un valle, é undio ciertos lugares de Indios, en que mureron hartos.

De dicho volcan ſalen muchas é muy buenas aguas, junto al dicho lugar de Nixapa ſe forma un rio dellas. I ſale un arroyo que corre i lleba agua de noche i aſta las 7 ú 8 del dia, é lo demas ſe zume é no pareze. Junto al cerro de San Juan, en la provincia de la Choluteca, es público ay otro que ſolo corre aſta medio dia, i de alli haſta la noche ſe zume el agua; i otra en la provincia de Chiapa que tres años continuos corre, i tres no corre ni parece agua.

Anſimiſmo en la falda de dicha volcan ay una oya redonda de mucha anchura que mueſtra haber ſido volcan i ardido mucho tiempo, porque en todo ſu circuyto la tierra i peña eſtá muy quemada é molida del fuego. Naze agora en ella una fuente de boniſſima agua, de que ſe provehe el lugar de Cuſcatan, que eſtá aſentado á la orilla della.

Junto al dicho lugar eſtá la ciudad de San Salvador; es de buen temple i fertil tierra, i en el altura de 13° 36′. Quando llegué á ella caſi eſtaba deſpoblada, porque un temblor grande que hizo el ſegundo dia de la Paſcua del Eſpiritu Santo paſado les derrocó i molió todas ſus caſas, que aunque muchas heran fuertes é buenas ſe cayeron é habrieron. Fue el mas eſpantoſo que jamas diceſe ha viſto.

Yo ví un lienzo bien grueſo de la pared de una Igleſia que habiendole lebantado el temblor

wide circumference, which is now extinct, probably becaufe it confumed all the materials of a combuftible nature which were in it, during the period of its activity. It has an enormous crater, half a league broad, and very deep. In defcending into it, are found two terraces or platforms, fimilar to thofe in lime kilns. From the laft and loweft rifes a fmoke fo offensive, that a Spaniard who reached there barely efcaped fuffocation. This mountain is covered from top to bottom with great cedars, pines, and forefts of other trees, abounding with animals, and has many deep ravines, caufed by fire.

Three leagues diftant, near a place named Nixapa, there is a piece of rough country called *malpays*, covered with rocks and burned earth in confufed maffes, which is the more furprifing as between this fpot and the volcano there is not the leaft trace of fire. ([18]) It muft be believed therefore, that thefe maffes were thrown here from the volcano, during one of its eruptions, as has happend with the volcano of Guatemala, which has vomited great volumes of fire within the paft few years, and as has happened alfo, in Nicaragua, where one broke out in eruption, and raifed feveral mountains in what was before a valley, overwhelming various Indian towns, and deftroying many of their inhabitants. There flow from this volcano a great many ftreams of water, which unite near the faid village of Nixapa, and form a river. There is one rivulet which flows all night, and until 7 or 8 o'clock

arriba, ſe tornó á ſentar deſbiado de ſu cimiento un xeme por algunas partes, y otras muchas coſas à eſte tono, i en el camino i ſierras que llaman de los Tecçacuangos hendidas por muchas partes. Ninguna coſa de los Indios de aquellas ſierras quedo en pie; todas cayeron. Contome un Eſpañol que caminaba por alli á la ſazon que tembló, que las ſierras pareciaſe juntaban, unas con otras, é que à el fue forzado á apearſe i tenderſe en el ſuelo, por que no ſe pudo tener en pie.

La caſa donde yo eſtaba arſaba como un navio; parecia que los demas llegaban con los tejados al ſuelo; é quiſo N. S. que no peligraron ſino tres perſonas que fue eſpanto i miſericordia ſuya; ſegun las caſas cayeron i la gente andaba turbada, i eſpantada en los arrabales de la ciudad.

Salen tres hojos muy grandes de agua caliente, muy buena i clara, é ſin ningun mal ſabor, i que en ſacandola ſe enfria i bebe; en ſu nacimiento es algo calida, aunque ſe puede ſufrir, como va corriendo ſe va resfriando. No creo que en el mundo puede haber diſpoſicion para los baños que en las dichas fuentes.

Cerca á la dicha ciudad ay una laguna, que boxa cinco leguas, de poco fructo haſta agora, aunque han hechado algunos mojarras, no havido peſcado de momento. Quentan los naturales Indios antiguos, que ſolia haver en ella culebras de eſtraña grandeza, i que un cazique de un lugar que ſe llama Atempamacegua topo una que ſegun la demoſtracion

in the morning, and which is dry during the reſt of the day. It is well known that near the mountains of San Juan, in the province of Choluteca, there is another ſpring which flows until noon, and then ſtops until night; and another in the province of Chiapas, in which the water flows for three years, and then ſtops for an equal time. ([19])

On the flank of the ſame volcano, is a large round opening, which appears to have been anciently a crater, for all around it the cliffs and earth are burned and cracked by fire. A ſmall ſtream of excellent water now flows from it, which ſupplies the village of Cuzcatlan, ſituated on its banks. Near here is the city of San Salvador, with a fine climate and fertile ſoil. Its latitude is 13° 36′. When I arrived there I found it nearly depopulated, in conſequence of a great earthquake which took place on the ſecond day of Eaſter preceding. This earthquake ſplit and threw down all the houſes of the town, notwithſtanding that they were generally ſtrong and well-built. It is ſaid that it was the ſevereſt and moſt fearful ever known. I myſelf ſaw a large fragment of the façade of a church, which had been lifted up, turned, and thrown for ſome diſtance from its foundation, and many other things of this kind. The road and the mountains called Tecçacuangos was fiſſured in many places, and not a ſingle houſe of the Indians in thoſe mountains was left ſtanding; all were thrown down. A Spaniard who was travelling

hacia debia tener mas que 50 pies. No lo tengo por cosa muy autentica, porque nadie dice la ha visto sino esta cazique, aunque es notorio por la fama antigua en toda aquella provincia.

En la costa del Sur ay unos campos que se llaman de Jivoga [Jiboa], que corren 14 leguas, hasta el rio Lempa, termino de la provincia de San Miguel, llanos y abundantes de pasto para gran cantidad de ganado; al presente ay algunas estancias, pero muy poco ganado para lo que podria haber. Ay en ella grandes pesquerias i disposicion para hacer sal al modo de los Indios. A un lado dellos, é á la falda de un alto volcan, estan quatro lugares de Indios que llaman los Nunualcos, donde de poco tiempo á esta parte se beneficia é cria cacao abundantisimamente, y en tanta cantidad que tanto por tanto escede a la provincia de los Izalcos.

A la parte del norte del dicho volcan está un lugar que se dize Iztepeque, i en sus terminos unos manantiales de agua caliente de la misma forma que dixe los habia en el lugar de Aguachapa; tienan mucho alumbre i azufre; en todo aquel alderredor ay muchos arboles i yerbas para buenos efectos, i en especial estan los montes llenos de la rayz de Mechoacan. Del lugar dicho, aunque es en la misma provincia, comienza otra lengua de Indios, que llaman los Chontales, gente mas bruta, aunque antiguamente valientes entre ellos.

Hay en la dicha provincia una laguana que se dize de Uxaca grande, i que de su desaguadero se

there, at the time, related to me, that the mountains rocked towards each other as if they would join, and that he was forced to diſmount and lie down, from the abſolute impoſſibility of ſtanding erect. The houſe in which I ſtopped, had been toſſed about like a veſſel at ſea, and it ſeems that the others were all thrown down with their roofs flat on the ground; but thanks to God only three perſons periſhed, which was a ſpecial mark of mercy, ſince moſt of the houſes fell while yet the inhabitants wandered in confuſion and alarm in the ſuburbs. ([20])

There are, near the city, three large ſprings of hot water, clear and good, without any bad taſte whatever, which may be drunk when it cools. They are of ſupportable temperature near their ſources, and the water cools in running, ſo that I do not believe there exiſts a better place in the world for the eſtabliſhment of baths, than is afforded by theſe ſprings. Near this city there is alſo a lake, about five leagues in circuit, but of very little utility, for although ſome *mojarras* have been thrown into it, yet up to this time it has no fiſh worthy of mention. The old Indians ſay that there are ſerpents in this lake, of extraordinary ſize, and that the cazique of a town called Atempamacegua encountered one which, according to his deſcription, was fifty feet long. I do not hold this as very authentic, for no one pretends having ſeen any, except this cazique; nevertheleſs the notion has prevailed in the country for a long time. ([21])

forma i haze el rio de Lempa, que es uno de los mayores deſte diſtricto. Tiene en medio dos peñoles, en uno de los quales antiguamente los Indios de aquel deſtricto hacia ſus ſacrificios e idolatrias. Es tierra aunque caliente, fertil, de mucha peſca i caza; hay algunos venados blancos, i no ſe ſabe en eſtas provincias en otras partes do los haya. En ſu ribera hay un jenero de arboles pequeños que dan una goma de lindo olor i que ſemeja i parece menjuy finiſimo; de la flor muy oloroſa i el fruto no ſe ſabe que ſea de provecho.

Tres leguas della eſta el lugar de Micla,* donde antiguamente los Indios Pipiles deſta diſtricto tenian gran devocion i venian á ofrecer ſus dones é hacer ſacrificios; i lo meſmo hazian los Chontales é otros Indios comarcanos de diferentes lenguas. Tenian en ſus ſacrificios algunas eſpecialidades que en otras partes, i *cues* i *teupas* de mucha autoridad, de que aun oy ay grandes ſeñales é indicios.

Allende del cazique i Señor natural, tenian un papá que llamaban *Tecti*, el qual ſe veſtia de una ropa larga azul, i traia en la cabeza una diadema i á vezes mitra labrada de diferentes colores, i en los cabos della un manojo de plumas muy buenas de unas pajaros que ay en eſta tierra, que llaman *Quetzales*. Traya de ordinario un báculo en la mano á manera de obiſpo, i à eſte obedecian todos

---

* Herrara, in copying this paragraph, ſubſtitutes *Mimilla* for *Micla*.

On the ſouth coaſt there is a plain called that of Jivoga [Jiboa], extending fourteen leagues to the river Lempa, which is the boundary of the province of San Miguel. It is level, abundant in paſturage, and capable of ſupporting a great number of cattle; but, at preſent, there are only a few farms, with but few cattle compared with what there might be. There are here ſome large fiſheries, and manufactures of ſalt, after the Indian faſhion. To one ſide, and on the flank of a high volcano [San Vicente], are four villages of Nunualco Indians, who have lately commenced the cultivation of cacao trees, which produce abundantly, and on equal ſpace of ground, even more than in the province of Izalco To the north of this volcano is a village called Iztepeque, near which are ſprings of hot water like thoſe of Aguachapa. Much alum and ſulphur is found here, and in the foreſts thereabouts are many trees and plants having medicinal virtues. They eſpecially abound in the root of Michoacan. At this place, although in the ſame province, the Indians commence to ſpeak a new language, called the Chontal. They are a very rude people, but had anciently a great reputation for valor amongſt their neighbors. ([22])

In this province there is a lake called Uxaca, in which the river Lempa, one of the largeſt in theſe regions, has its ſource. It has in its center two high rocky iſlands, on one of which the Indians formerly made their ſacrifices and practiced their idolatries. The diſtrct around the lake, although

en lo que tocaba a las cosas espirituales. Despues de deste tenia el segundo lugar en el sacerdozio otro que llaman *tehu a matlini* que hera el mayor echizero i letrado en sus libros i artes, i el que declaraba los agüeros i hacia sus pronosticos. Habia allende destos quatro sacerdotes que llamaban *teupixqui* vestidos de diferentes colores i de ropas hasta sus pies, negras, verdes, colorados, i amarillas; i estos heran los del consejo de las cosas de sus ceremonias, i los que asistian a todas los supersticiones i boberias de su gentilidad.

Habia tambien un mayordomo que tenia cuydado de guardar las joyas i preseas de sus sacrificios, i el que sacaba los corazones á los sacrificados, i hazia las demas cosas personales que heran necesarias; i sin los dichos habia otros que tenian trompetas é instrumentos de su gentilidad para convocar i llamar la gente á los sacrificios que habia de hazer.

Eleccion del Papá i Sacerdotes.

Quando el Papá fallecia, lo enterraban asentado en un banco pintado, en su propia casa, i le lloraba todo el pueblo quinze dias, con muchos gritos i alaridos; ayunaban todos los quinze dias; acabadas las obsequias, el cazique i el sabio elegian otro papa por suertes, i habia de ser uno de los quatro sacerdotes susodichos; i à la elecion deste hacian grandes *mitotes* i fiestas, i este electo sacrificaba la lengua i

ſomewhat hot, is fertile, and abounds in fiſh and game. There are white deer alſo, which, ſo far as I know, are not to be found elſewhere. On its ſhores is a kind of ſmall tree, which yields a gum of delicate odor, reſembling the fineſt *benjamin;* and alſo a flower of great ſweetneſs, but I do not know if the fruit be good or of uſe. (23)

Three leagues diſtant, is the village of Micla, which anciently the Pipil Indians of this diſtrict held in great veneration; it was here they came to make their offerings and ſacrifices, as did alſo the Chontals, and other neighboring Indians of different languages. Their modes of ſacrificing differed in ſome reſpects from thoſe of other parts. They had *cues* or temples, and *teupas* or prieſts of high authority, of which there are ſtill many ſigns and traces.

Beſides their cazique or ſecular lord, they had a kind of pope, called *Tecti*, who dreſſed in a long blue robe, and wore on his head a diadem, or ſometimes a mitre embroidered with many colors, at the crown of which roſe a cluſter of very beautiful feathers, taken from a bird, called in this country, *Quetzal.* (24) This pontiff carried in his hand a ſtaff, which reſembled the crook of a biſhop, and he was obeyed in all ſpiritual things. After him, next in ſacerdotal authority, was the *tehu a matlini*, who was the ableſt diviner and the man beſt verſed in their ancient books and in their arts. He it was who made auguries and foretold future events. After him, were four prieſts called *teupixquis*, who

miembro genital i la ſangre ofrecia á ſus idolos, i eſte elexia el ſacerdote que habia de entrar en ſu lugar, i havia de ſer uno de los hijos del papa muerto ſi los tenia u otro hijo de los ſacerdotes, i los demas oficios que faltaba en ſus *teupas*.

Adoraban el ſol quando ſale, i tenian dos idolos, el uno en figura de hombre, i eſte ſe llamaba *Quetzalcoatl*, i el otro en figura de muger, *Itzqueye*; todos los ſacrificios que hacian heran à los ſuſodichos, i tenian calendarios ó dias diputados para cada uno dellos, i anſi el ſacrificio ſe hazia conforme á quien caya la ſuerte del dia.

Sacrificios.

Hacian dos ſacrificios ſolenes cada año, el uno al principio del invierno, i otro al principio del verano; i eſte ſacrificio hera dentro de la caſa de oracion, i los que ſacrificaban para eſte ſacrificio heran muchachos de ſeis años haſta doce, baſtardos, i nacidos entre ellos.

La Manera deſte Sacrificio.

Tañian ſus trompetas i atabales un dia i una noche antes, i luego todo el pueblo ſe juntaba en la manera ſuſodicha, i los quatro ſacerdotes dichos ſalian del *cue* con quartro braſeritos de fuego, i en

went dreſſed in long robes, falling to their feet, each of different color, black, red, green and yellow. Theſe were the counſellors of the pontiff, and directed all the ſuperſtitious ceremonies and follies of their religion. There was alſo a kind of *mayordomo,* who had charge of the ſacred jewels and the inſtruments of ſacrifice. He alſo opened the breaſts of the victims of ſacrifice, and tore out their hearts, and performed ſuch other perſonal ſervices as were requiſite. Beſides all theſe there were other functionaries, who played on the drums, trumpets and other inſtruments uſed in convoking the people to the ſacrifices.

Election of the Pope and Prieſts.

When the chief prieſt died, he was buried in his own houſe, ſeated in a painted chair, and all the people mourned for him for fifteen days, with loud cries and lamentations. They alſo faſted during this period; but when this was over, the cazique and the wiſe man or diviner ſelected a new pontiff by lot. It was requiſite that he ſhould be one of the four prieſts above mentioned. When the choice was made, they had great feaſts and dances, and he who was choſen drew blood from his tongue and private parts, and offered it in ſacrifice to the idols. He alſo named his ſucceſſor in the prieſthood, who was required to be a ſon of the deceaſed pontiff, if he had left one, if not, the ſon of ſome other prieſt. He filled alſo the other offices which at any time

ellos pueſtos copal i ule, ivanſe derechos todos quatro juntos á do ſale el ſol, i ſe hincavan de rodillas ante el, i le zaumavan diciendo palabras é invocaciones, i eſto fecho ſe dividian hacia quatro partes, leſt, oeſt, norte, ſur, i predicavan ſus riƈtos i ceremonias. Acavado el ſermon ſe entravan coriendo en unas caſas que tenia hechá los quatros vientos, i deſcanſavan un rato. De ay ſe iban á la caſa del papa que eſtava junto al *cu*, i alli tomavan el muchacho que havian de ſacrificar, i davan quatro bueltas al patio en manera de baile cantando. Acabadas las bueltas ſalia el papa de ſu caſa, con el ſabio i mayordomo, i ſubian al *cu* con el cazique i principales, los quales quedavan á la puerta de ſu adoratario, i luego los quatro ſacerdotes tomavan al muchacho en brazos, cada uno de ſu mano i pie; i ſalian luego al mayordomo con caſcaveles en los pies i manos, i moijado, i por el ſinieſtro lado le ſacavan el corazon i lo davan al papa, el qual lo ponia en una bolſa labrada pequeña i la cerra, i los quatro ſacerdotes tomavan la ſangre del ſacrificado en unas quartro jicaras, que ſon vaſos de cierta fruta que los Indios uſan, i ſalian uno tras otro, abajavan al patio, i á las quarto partes de los vientos dichos aſperjavan la ſangre con la mano derecha; i ſi ſobrava algun ſangre, la volvian adonde eſtava el papa, el qual hechava la ſangre, corazon i bolſa en el cuerpo del ſacrificado por la propia herida, i enterravanlo en el miſmo

became vacant in the *teupas*, or temples. They adored the riſing ſun, and had two idols, one repreſenting a man, whom they called *Quetzalcoatl*, and the other a woman named *Itzqueye*. All their ſacrifices were made to them, and they had a calendar, with days ſpecially ſet apart for each one, and on theſe the ſacrifices were made.

Sacrifices.

Each year they had two principal and very ſolemn ſacrifices; one at the commencement of ſummer, and the other at the beginning of winter. Theſe were made in the interior of the ſacred place or temple, and were of boys between the ages of six and twelve years, baſtards, born among themſelves.

Mode of theſe Sacrifices.

They ſounded their trumpets and drums for one day and night before the ſacrifice, and when the people were aſſembled, the four prieſts came out from the temple, with four ſmall braziers in which they burnt copal and caoutchouc; and the four together, turning in the direction of the riſing sun, bent their knees to it, offering incenſe, and reciting words of invocation. After this they ſeparated, and did the ſame in the direction of the four cardinal points, ſouth, eaſt, north and weſt, preaching and explaining their rites and ceremonies. When the ſermon was finiſhed, they retired within four houſes or chapels which were built at the four corners of

cue. Eſte era el ſacrificio que hacian por los tiempos del año.

Juntavanſe el papa, ſabio i hechizero, con ſus quatro ſacerdotes i ſabian por ſus ſuertes i hechicerias ſi harian guerra ó ſi alguno venia contra ellos, i ſi las ſuertes les decian que ſi, llamavan al cazique i capitanes de guerra, i decianles como venian los enemigos é adonde havian de ir á hazer guerra. El cazique apercevia todà ſu gente de guerra i ſalia en buſca de ſus enemigos, i ſi tenian victoria en la batalla, luego el cazique deſpachava correo al papa, i le haviſava el dia que havia ſubcedido, i el ſabio via aquien ſe havia de hacer el ſacrificio. Si era á *Quetzalcoatl*, durava el *mitote* 15 dias, i cada dia ſacrifican un Indio de los que havian cautivado en la batalla; i ſi era á *Itzqueye* durava el *mitote* cinco dias, i cada dia ſacrificavan otro Indio.

El ſacrificio ſe hacia en eſta manera; que todos los que ſe hallaron en la guerra venian en ordenanza cantando i bailando, i traian á los que havian de ſacrificar con muchas plumas i *chalchivetes* à los pies i manos con ſartas de cacao al peſcuezo, i eſtas traian los capitanes en medio de ſi. Salia el papa i ſacerdotes con los demas del pueblo á recebillos con baile i muſica, i los caziques i capitanes ofrecían al papa, aquellos Indios para el ſacrificio, ivanſe luego todos juntos al patio de ſu *teupa* i bailavan todos los dias i noches ſuſodichos. I en medio del patio ponian una piedra como poyo, i ſobre ella hechaban al

the temple, and there rested for a little while. They next went to the house of the high priest, which was close to the temple, and took thence the boy who was to be sacrificed, and conducted him four times around the court of the temple, dancing and singing. When the ceremony was finished, the high priest came out of his house, with the second priest and mayordomo, and ascended the steps of the temple, accompanied by the cazique and principal Indians, who, however, stopped at the door of the sanctuary. The four priests next seized the victim by his extremities, and the mayordomo coming out, with little bells on his wrists and ankles, opened the left breast of the boy, tore out his heart and handed it to the high priest, who put it into a little embroidered purse, which he closed. The priests received the blood of the victim in four *jicaras*, which are vessels made from the shell of a certain kind of fruit (the *calabash*), and, descending one after another into the court, sprinkled it, with their right hands, in the direction of the cardinal points. If any blood remained over, they returned it to the high priest, who put it back, with the purse containing the heart, into the body of the victim, which was interred in the temple itself. This was the kind of sacrifice made at the opening of the two seasons of the year. (25)

The high priest, his second, and the four priests were accustomed to meet to ascertain, by sorcery and enchantment, if they should make war, or if

Indio que habian de ſacrificar deſpaldas i los quatro ſacerdotes tenian al Indio de pies i manos, ſalia el mayordomo con muchas plumas i cargado de caſcabeles con un navajon de piedra en la mana, i le abria el pecho, i le ſacaba el corazon, i en ſacandolo lo hechaba en alto á las partes de los quatro vientos, i la quinta vez lo echaba en medio del patio derecho en alto quanto podia i decia toma Dios el premio deſta vitoria. Eſte ſacriſicio hera publico que todos chicos i grandes lo vian.

Los que heran ſoldados de la guerra no dormian en ſus caſas çon ſus mugeres ſino en unos *calpules* que tenian diputados por ellos, lo propio los manzebos que amoſtraban elarte de la milicia, i de dia iban á caſas de ſus mugeres á comer i beber, i de allí á ſus milpas, i ſiempre quedava una compañia á guardar el pueblo. Conocianſe los valientes en el que mas agujeros ſe haria en ſu miembro, aquel hera mas valiente. Las mugeres ſacrificavan las orejas i lengua, i ſe labravan todo el cuerpo, i la ſangre que le ſalia lo coxian en algodones i lo ofrecian á ſus idoles, las mugeres á *Itzqueye*, i los hombres á *Quetzalcoatl.*

Las ſuperſticiones que hazian para ſus ſementeras hera que tomávan en unas jicaras pequeñas todas las ſuertes de ſemillas que querian ſembrar, i las llevaban ante el altar de ſus idolos, i en el ſuelo hazian un oyo, i los ponian por ſu horden i la cobijaban con tierra, i ſobre ellos ponian un braſero grande con muchas braſas i con copal y ule. I los

their foes were coming to attack them; and if it appeared that ſuch an event was to take place, they called together the cazique and war chief, and adviſed them of the approach of their enemies, and whether they ſhould go to meet them. The cazique then aſſembled the ſoldiers, and all went out to battle. If he was victorious, he deſpatched a meſſenger to the high prieſt, adviſing him of the date of the occurrence, and on this information the diviner aſcertained to which of the Gods ſacrifice was to be made. If to *Quetzálcoatl*, the ceremonies laſted fifteen days; if to *Itzqueye*, five days, and on each day they ſacrificed a priſoner. Theſe ſacrifices were made as follows: All thoſe who had taken part in the war, returned home in order, ſinging and dancing, and bringing with them thoſe who were to be ſacrificed, decorated with feathers and *chalchiuites* on their wriſts and ankles, and with ſtrings of cacao beans around their necks, the captains themſelves conducting them in their midſt. The pontiff and prieſts, at the head of the people, went out to meet the victors, with muſic and dancing; and when they encountered them, the captains delivered over the victims to be ſacrificed to the high prieſt; after which all went together to the court of their *teupa*, where they kept up the dancing night and day, for the periods above named. In the middle of this court was placed a block or bench of ſtone, on which the victim was ſtretched, the four prieſts holding him

quatro ſacerdotes ſacrificaban las orejas i narizes, i por ellas ſe metian unas cañas largas i las quemaban ante ſus Idolos. I otras vezes ſacaban ſangre de la lengua i miembro, i pedian á ſus idolos les dieren fruƈtas i que fruƈtificaren todas las ſemilas de la tierra. El papa ſe ſacrificaba la lengua i orejas, i miembro, i la ſangre que deſta ſalia untaba pies i manos á los idolos, é invocaba al demonio i hablaba con el, i les decian los tiempos que habian de ſubceder i mandaba á aquellos quatro ſacerdotes, dijeſen al pueblo lo que el idolo le habia dicho, i ſiempre concluian eſta platica con mandalles que tubieſen comunicacion con ſus mugeres, i de alli fueſen á ſembrar; i eſto hera el ſacrificio de ſemillas.

Lo que hazian en los ſacrificios de la peſca i caza hera que tomaban un venado vivo, i llevabánlo al patio del *cue* é egleſia que tenian fuera del pueblo, i lo aogaban i lo deſollaban, i le ſalvaban toda la ſangre en una olla, i el higado, i bofes, i buches lo hazian pedazos muy menudos, i el corazon, cabeza, i pies; apartaban i mandaban cozer el venado por ſi, i la ſangre por ſi, i mientras eſto ſe cozia hacian ſu bayle. Tomaban el Papa i ſabio la cabeza del venado por las orejas, i los quatro ſacerdotes los quatro pies, i el mayordomo en un braſero llevaba el corazon ſe quemavan con ule i copal, é inſenſaba al idolo que tenian pueſto i ſeñalado para la caza i peſca. Acabado el *mitote* ofrecian la cabeza i pies al idolo i chamuſcabanla, i deſpues de chamuſcado la llevaban á caſa del papa i ſe la comia, i el venado

by the feet and hands. The ſacrificer then came forward, loaded with plumes and bells, with a knife of flint, with which he opened the breaſt of the victim, and took out his heart, and toſſed it in the air in the direction of the four cardinal points, and finally threw it aloft directly in the middle of the court, in this way ſoliciting the divinity to accept the ſacrifice, in return for the victory. This ſacrifice was public to all the Indians, great and ſmall.

During this period, the ſoldiers returning from the war, could not cohabit with their wives, but were obliged to ſleep in certain *calpules* or barracks, which were given up to them for the occaſion, by the young men who were learning the art of war. ([26]) During the day they went to the houſes of their women to eat and drink, and from thence to their plantations, always however leaving a company to guard the town. The men ſacrified blood drawn from their private parts, and he who had moſt wounds in theſe was reputed to be moſt valiant. The women ſacrificed blood drawn from their tongues and ears, and they sacrified their entire bodies, taking up the blood with cotton and offering it to their idols—the men to *Quetzalcoatl*, and the women to *Itzqueye*.

Their ſuperſtitious ceremonies, at the time of planting their fields, were as follows: They put in little cups of calabaſh the ſeeds which they had ſelected for the purpoſe, and placed them before

i ſangre comian delante del idolo, u otro qualquier animal que ſacrificaſen, i á los peſcados lo ſacaban las tripas i lo quemaban ante el dicho idolo; lo propio hera en los demas animales.

Lo que uſaban quando parian las mugeres, que llamado á la partera la preñada no podia parir, luego le hazian dezir ſus pecados i ſi no paria, hazia que ſe confeſaſe el marido, i ſi no podia con eſto, ſi havia dicho i confeſado que conoſia alguno, ivan á caſa de aquel i traian de ſu caſa la manta é pañetes i ceiñola á la preñada paraque pariese; i ſi no baſtara, el marido ſacrificara las orejas i lengua. Quando la criatura nacia, ſi era hombre le ponian un arco i flechas en la mano, i ſi era muger un uſo i algodon, i la partera le hacia en el pie derecho una raya con tizne ſignificava, eſta raya que quando fueſe grande no ſe perdieſen por los montes. Paſando doze dias llevaban la criatura al ſacerdote, i aquel que la llebava le cortarban ramos verdes en que piſaſe; i llegado ante el ſacerdote le ponia el nombre de ſus aguelos ó aguelas, i le ofrecian cacao ó gallinas, i eſtas eran las ofrendas de las ſacerdotes. Llegados á caſa con la criatura la partera tomaba á la recienparida i la llebava á lavar al rio, i ofrecia al agua cacao i copal, i eſto hacian porque el agua no le hicieſe mal.

Los ricτos de ſus difunctos eran que ſi fallecia el Caçique ó algun Capitan ó Señor, ó hijo, ó muger deſtos, los llorava todo el pueblo quatro dias i quatro noches; á la quarta noche quando amanecia

the altar of their idols. They next dug a trench in the ground, in which they planted the ſeeds regularly, covering them with earth; and over all they placed a large brazier, full of burning coals, on which they ſprinkled copal and caoutchouc. The four prieſts then drew blood from their ears and noſe, receiving it in certain large reeds, which they burnt before their idols. At other times they drew blood from their tongues and private members, and petitioned their gods to proſper the fruits of the earth, and give them abundant harveſts. The high prieſt, in ſacrificing, drew blood from the ſame parts, and with it anointed the feet and hands of the idols, invoking the demon, who ſpoke with him, and told him what kind of weather would follow, all of which was communicated to the people by the four prieſts, who always concluded by ordering the men to have connection with their wives, and then proceed to plant their fields. And ſuch was the ſacrifice of planting.

We came now to their ſacrifices for hunting and fiſhing. They took a living deer to the courtyard of the *cue* or temple which they had outſide of the town, where they ſtrangled and ſkinned him, collecting all his blood in a vaſe, and cutting in ſmall pieces the liver, lungs and ſtomach. Theſe were put aſide, with the heart, head, and feet. They next cut up and cooked the deer by itſelf, and the blood by itſelf, and while theſe were cooking they had their dances. Next the high prieſt and his

ſalia el papa i decia que el anima de aquel Caçique eſtava con los Dioſes i que no lloraſen mas; eſtos todos ſe enterravan en ſus propias caſas, aſentados i veſtidos con todos ſus bienes, i aquellas quatro noches y dias ſu llorar era como á manera de *mitote*, cantavan ſus hazañas i linajes. Si era cazique luego otro dia el papa i todos los demas del pueblo tomavan por Señor al hijo ó hija ſi los tenia, i ſi no, al hermano ó pariente mas cercano. I á la eleccion deſte ſe hacian grandes fieſtas i bailes i ſacrificios, i el dava de comer á todos los capitanes i ſacerdotes en ſu caſa. Si el difunto no era de principal, ſolo ſus parientes le lloravan i ſus hijos; i ſi alguna muger ſe le moria la criatura, guardava la leche quatro dias que no la dava á ninguna otra criatura, porque tenian por agüero que el difunto le havia algun daño ó mal; eſte ſacrificio ſe llamava *navitia*.

El cazique era ſu oficio de mandar ſembrar i caſar á los Indios, i ſiempre los caſavan con muchachas, i quando eſtavan concertados, ſi acaſo el yerno encontrava al ſuégro, torcia el camino, lo propio hacia la nuera á la ſuegra; i hacian eſto porque el diablo les decia que no havrian hijos ſi ſe topavan con los ſuegros. El caſamiento i boda ſe hacia en eſta manera; que los parientes de la novia ivan por el novio, i lo llebavan al rio á lavar; i las parientas del novio ivan por la novia i lavados en el rio; ambos los enbolvian cada qual en ſu manta blanca nueva, i los llebavan á la caſa de la

aſſiſtant took the head by the ears, and each of the four prieſts one of the feet, and the mayordomo put the heart in a braſier and burned it, with copal and caoutchouc, as incenſe to the idol of the god who was held to be protector of hunting and fiſhing. When the dance was finiſhed, the head and feet were ſcorched in the fire before the idol, as an offering, and afterwards taken to the houſe of the high-prieſt and eaten. The fleſh and blood were then eaten before the idol; and the ſame was done with all the animals which they offered in ſacrifice. When they ſacrificed fiſh, the entrails were burnt before the idol. ([27])

When a woman was in travail, the midwives made her confess her ſins; but if this was not ſufficient to haſten the birth, they made her huſband do the ſame; and finally, if the woman admitted illicit connection with any other man, they went to his houſe and took his clothes and placed them beneath her; if this failed, as a laſt reſort, the huſband ſacrificed blood from his tongue and ears. When the child was born, if a boy, they put in his hands a bow and arrows; if a girl, a ſpindle of cotton; and the mother made a ſtreak of ſoot mixed with water on the right foot of the child, which they believed would prevent it, when grown up, from being loſt in the woods. At the end of twelve days, the child was taken to the prieſt, green branches being ſcattered under the feet of the bearers. The prieſt gave it the name of its grand-

novia, i los ataban juntos en las dos mantas añudadas desnudos en cueros; i los parientes del novio davan presentes á la novia, jicoles, mantas, algodon, gallinas, cacao, i los parientes de la novia lo mesmo al novio; i luego comian todos juntos, i á estos casamientos se hallavan el cazique i papa de necesidad.

En lo que tocava al parentesco, tenian un arbol pintado, i en el siete ramos que signifacava siete grados de parentesco. En estos grados no se podia casar nadie, i esto se entendia por linea recta si no fuese que alguno huviese fecho algun gran fecho en armas, i havia de ser del tercero grado fuera; i por linea traversa tenia otro arbol con quatro ramos que significaban el quarto grado, en estos no se podia casar nadie.

Fuera de otras leyes que los Indios tenian en toda esta provincia, tenian los desta nacion por inviolables las siguientes:

Qualquiera que menospreciava los sacrificios de sus Idolos ó rictos, moria por ello.

Qualquiera que se echava con muger ajéna moria por ello.

Qualquiera que tenia quenta carnal con parienta en los grados susodichos morian por ello ambos.

Qualquiera que hablara con qualquiera muger ó le hacia señas si era casada, le desterravan de su pueblo i la quitavan sus bienes.

Qualquiera que se echava con esclava ajena le hacian esclavo, sino fuese que la tal persona le per-

father or grandmother, as the caſe might be, and they preſented it with cacao and fowls, which were the offerings made to the prieſt. When it was taken back to the houſe, the mother carried it to a river and bathed it, offering to the ſtream cacao and copal, that it ſhould never do evil to the child.

As regards the rites for the dead; if the defunct were a cazique or captain, or the wife or child of either, all the people mourned for four days and nights. At the riſing of the ſun on the fifth day, the high prieſt announced that the ſoul of the dead was with the gods, and that it was uſeleſs to mourn any longer. They buried the dead man dreſſed in all of his riches, in a ſitting poſture, and in his own houſe. ([28]) Their manner of mourning during the four days and nights reſembled a *mitote*, in which they chaunted the lineage and deeds of the dead. If he were a cazique who died, the high prieſt and all the people, immediately recognized as his ſucceſſor his ſon or daughter; or, if he had neither, his brother or neareſt relative. On ſuch occaſions they had great feaſts, dances and ſacrifices, and the new chief entertained in his houſe all the prieſts and captains. If a common man died, only his children and relatives mourned; and if a woman loſt her child, ſhe reſerved her milk for four days, without giving it to another; for they believed, if ſhe failed in this, the dead child would do the living one ſome injury. This ſacrifice they called *navitia*.

donaſe el papa por ſervicios que huvieſe fecho en la guerra.

Qualquiera que hurtava hurto, como fueſe grave, moria por ello.

Qualquiera que forzava donçella le ſacrificavan por ello.

Qualquiera que mentia lo azotavan bravamente, i ſi era en coſa de guerra le hacian eſclavo por ello.

Loſ que no eran para la guerra, cultivaban las tierras millpas del cazique i papa i ſacerdotes, i de las propias ſuyas davan un tanto para la gente de guerra. Eſto es lo que he alcanzado deſte pueblo.

En el dicho lugar eſtá una peña de donde ſalen dos ojos de agua caſi juntos; el uno muy caliente i el otro frio.

Hay en el muchas eſpecias que los Indios uſan para ſu bebidas i comidas; é una tierra que parece caparoſa, que lo deve de ſer ſegun el efecto hace, con que ſe hace tinta. En toda eſta provincia, del comienza la provincia i correximiento del pueblo de Chiquimula de la Sierra, es la mas del tierra alta i de buen temple i paſtos, i fertil para labranzas i crianzas de todo jenero de mantemientos i ganado.

Acia la parte que deſte lugar van á Gracias á Dios en Honduras ſon Indios Chontales. Averigüé eſtando alli un delito contra un cacique del lugar de Gotera, el qual deſde ſu gentilidad tenia

It was the office of the cazique to order the plantings, and direct the marriages. They always married when young; and when the affair was arranged, and the affianced groom met his future father-in-law he turned aside, as also did the affianced bride when she met her future mother-in-law. They did this, because the devil had made them believe that such encounters would prevent their having children. Marriages were celebrated in this wise: the male relatives of the woman sought the bridegroom and made him bathe in a river; and the female relatives of the woman did the same with the bride; they then wrapped each of them in a new, white cloth, and took them to the house of the bride, where they tied them up naked, in their garments. The relatives of the young man then made presents to the bride of cloths, cottons, fowls and cacao, while those of the bride gave presents of the same kind to the bridegroom; after which they all feasted together. At these marriages the high priest and cazique were obliged to be present. ([29])

Concerning relationship: They have a tree painted, with seven branches, which represent the seven degrees of relationship in direct descent, within which no person might marry, excepting those who had distinguished themselves in war, but even these might not marry within three degrees of blood. In respect of the line collateral, they made use of another tree with four branches, which

el miembro hendido i abierto, que era una de las gentilidades usavan antiguamente los mas valientes. En aquel año de 1563, en otro lugar cercano que se llama Cezori ciertos Indios idolatraron en un monte en sus terminos, i entre ellos que uno se harpó i hendió su miembro, i que circuncidaron quatro muchachos de doze años para arriba al uso judaico, i la sangre que salio dellos la sacrificaron á un idolo de piedra redondo, llamado *Icelaca*, con dos caras atras i adelante, i con muchos ojos. Decian que este era el Dios que sabia lo presente i lo pasado, i via todas las cosas. Tenia untadas ambas caras i ojos con sangre, i sacrificaronle venados, gallinas, conejos, aji, chian, otras cosas que ellos usavan antiguamente.

Cerca del dicho lugar estava un cerro alto en la prespectiva, parece sabrepuja á todas las alturas comarcanas, i tiene en su alto una laguna de agua dulce, grande de mucha hondura, sin que parezca de donde puede tener vertiente ó nacer tanta agua; cierto que mirada la situacion de toda la tierra, parece que alli es lo mas alto dellos, é que ó la laguna es milagrosa, ó tiene algun venero que las hondas estrañas de la tierra que produce i sustenta de ordinario tan gran piélago de agua, i aun vertiente grande que de ella sale siempre. Crianse alli muchas dantas mas que en otra parte de aquella tierra, suelense matar algunas aunque la carne no es muy buena de comer porque es viscosa; tienen dos buches, en el uno hechan el pasto ordinario, i el

reprefented the four degrees within which no one could marry.

Afide from other laws which thefe Indians poffeffed in common throughout the province, thofe of this nation have the following as inviolable:

Whoever contemned or ridiculed the facrifices to the idols, or the ceremonies connected therewith, was condemned to death.

Whoever had connection with a ftrange woman, was condemned to death.

Thofe who had carnal intercourfe with relatives, within the degrees above profcribed, both fuffered death.

He who fpoke libidinoufly with a married woman, or who made improper figns to her, was banifhed and his property confifcated.

Whoever had commerce with a ftrange flave [one not his own?] was himfelf reduced to flavery, unlefs pardoned by the high prieft for fervices in war.

Whoever wounded another, if the wound were ferious, fuffered death therefor.

Whoever violated a virgin was facrificed.

Whoever lied was feverely whipped; and if it were in any matter concerning war, he was enflaved.

Thofe of the people who were not foldiers cultivated the plantations of the cazique, pontiff and priefts; and alfo gave a part of their own crops for the fupport of the warriors.

This is what I have been able to gather concerning the manners and cuftom of this people.

otro trae ſiempre lleno de palos i madera podrida; no ſe que ſea de algun efecto, mas es de creer que no ſe lo diló naturaleza de valde.

En la provincia dicha eſté un lugarejo encomendado en un Geronimo Italiano; ſucedió allí el año de 1764, que canſados los Indios i enfadados de una larga enfermedad que havia tenido ſu cazique, de acuerdo i juntos fueron á ſu caſa i le dixeſon que ſegun ſu enfermidad havia ſido larga, eſtavan canſados de ſerville, i que pues ya no era de provecho, ni los podia governar ſe muriefe i acavaſe de dalles mas peſadumbre; el cazique enfermo les reſpondió que tenian razon, i pues anſi era que el ſe queria morir que lo enterraran; i ellos oida ſu determinacion lo amortajaron vivo i tocaron á muerto i lo llevaron á enterrar, occurrieron á la igleſia los mas del lugar i entre ellos la muger del encomendero, i admirada que eſtando el dicho cazique poco antes con mediana diſpoſicion ſe huviere muerto tan preſto, ſe llego à el é dijo á las Indios que no le enterraren que podria ſer algun deſmayo, i como tentando le vio que eſtava caliente, quitóle el velo del roſtro i vióle vivo, i ella riñendo á los que lo llevaban á enterrar, le quitó de allí i llevó á ſu caſa i vivió deſpues mas de quatro meſes, é para deſeno jalla le decia el cazique i los vecinos que peor huviera ſido ſi lo mataran. Eſta muger del dicho encomendero por el año de 64 ſe hizo preñada é malpario cinco hijos de una vez, de cinco meſes i todos vivos.

Near this place, is a high rocky hill from which flow two ſtreams of water, cloſe to each other, one hot and the other cold. Here too is found an abundance of ſpices, which the Indians uſe in their drink and food; and an earth which reſembles copperas, and which it muſt be judging from its effects. With this they make a dye.

From here to the borders of the province of Chiquimula de la Sierra, the country is for the moſt part high, of good temperature, abounding in paſturage, and adapted for the ſupport of cattle, and the cultivation of all kinds of grains.

In the portion of this province which lies in the direction of Gracias á Dios in Honduras, are the Chontal Indians. While there, complaint was made to me againſt a cazique of a place called Gotera, who ſince the time of his paganiſm had had his private member ſplit open, as was the cuſtom anciently, among the moſt valiant. In 1563, certain idolatrous Indians of another village called Cezori, got together in a neighboring foreſt where one of them performed the ſame operation; and afterwards they circumciſed four boys of twelve years of age, in the Jewiſh manner, offering the blood to an idol of ſtone of a cylindrical form, with a double viſage and many eyes, called *Icelaca*. They ſay that he is the God which knows the preſent and the paſt, and ſees all things. Both his faces were anointed with blood, and they ſacrificed to him deer, fowls, rabbits, peppers, and other things which they uſed in ancient times.

Ruinas de Copan.

Cerca del dicho lugar como van á la ciudad de San Pedro, en el primer lugar de la provincia de Honduras, que ſe llama Copan, eſtan unas ruinas i veſtijios de gran poblacion i de ſobervios edificios, i tales que parece que en ningun tiempo pudo haver, en tan barbaro injenio como tienen los naturales de aquella provincia, edificio de tanta arte i ſuntuoſidad; es ribera de un hermoſo rio, i en unos campos bien ſituados i eſtendidos, tierra de mediano temple, harta de fertilidad, é de mucha caza é peſca.

En las ruinas dichas, hai montes que parecen haver ſido fechos á manos, i en ellos muchas coſas de notar. Antes de llegar á ellos, eſtá ſeñal de paredes grueſas i una piedra grandiſima en figura de aguila, i fecho en ſu pecho un quadro de largo de una vara, i en el ciertas letras que no ſe ſabe que ſea.

Llegados á las ruinas, eſtá otra piedra en figura de gigante; dicen los Indios antiguas que era la guarda de aquel Santuario; entrando en el ſe halló una cruz de piedra de tres palmos de alto, con un brazo quebrado.

Mas adelante van ciertas ruinas i algunas piedras en ellas labradas con harto primor; i eſtá una eſtatua grande de mas que quatro varas de alto, labrada como un obiſpo veſtido de pontifical, con ſu mitro bien labrada i anillos en las manos. Junto á

From here, in the diſtance, is ſeen a very high mountain, which ſeems to riſe above all the others. It has at its top a lake of ſweet water, very deep. It is difficult to conceive whence the water comes, ſince the mountain appears to overlook all the land, and to be the higheſt in it; and it is a queſtion whether the lake is miraculous, or has ſome ſource within its depths in the earth which ſupplies it with ſo much water that a ſtream flows from it conſtantly. There are produced here many tapirs, more than in any other part of the country. The Indians ſometimes kill them, but their fleſh is not very good for food. This animal has two ſtomachs; in one is found the ordinary graſs which he eats, but the other is always full of branches of trees and fine pieces of wood. I know not what may be the uſe of this, but it may well be believed that nature has not given it without a purpoſe.

In the ſaid province there is a ſmall place, which is aſſigned to one Geronimo Italiano, and here it happened, in the year 1574, that the Indians wearied and irritated by the long illneſs of their cazique, went in a body to his houſe, and informed him that his long infirmity had made them tired of ſerving and ſupporting him, and that being himſelf unable to do any good or to govern them, he had better die, and thus relieve them from further trouble. The chief replied that they had cauſe for what they ſaid, and that he was willing to die at

ella eſtá una plaza muy bien fecha con ſus grados à la forma que eſcriben del Coliſeo Romano, i por algunas partes tiene ochenta gradas, enloſada i labrada por cierto en partes de mui buena piedra é con harto primor; eſtá en ella ſeis eſtatuas grandiſimas, las tres de hombres armados á lo moſaico con ligagambas, é ſembradas muchas labores por las armas, i las otras dos de mugeres con buen ropaje largo i tocaduras á lo Romano; la otra es de obiſpo que parece tener en las manos un bulto como cofrecito. Devian de ſer idolos, porque delante de cada una dellas havia una piedra grande que tenia fecha una pileta con ſu ſumidero donde degollavan los ſacrificados i corria la ſangre; tambien tenian ſendas cazolejas do ſacrificavan con ſus ſahumerios, i en medio de la plaza havia otro pila mayor que parece de bautizar, donde anſimeſmo devian de hazer en comun ſus ſacrificios. Paſada eſta plaza ſe ſube por muchas gradas á un promontorio alto que devia de ſer donde hacian ſus *mitotes* i rictos; parece fue fecho i labrado con mucha curioſidad, porque aun ſiempre ſe hallan alli piedras muy bien labradas. A un lado deſte edificio parece una torre ó terrapleno alto que cae ſobre el rio, que por alli paſa; haſe caido i derrumbado un gran pedazo, i en lo caido ſe deſcubrieron dos cuevas debajo del dicho edificio muy largas i angoſtas, i fechos con harta curioſidad; no he podido averiguar de que ſervian é para que ſe hicieron; hay una eſcalera que baja haſta el rio por muchas

once, if they would bury him. He then fainted away or ſeemed to die, and taking him for dead, they carried him off for burial. Moſt of the people of the place gathered at the funeral, and among them the wife of Geronimo, who wondered how it was that the chief, who was before only a little indiſpoſed, ſhould be dead ſo ſoon. She accordingly told the Indians that they muſt not bury him, as he might be in a ſwoon. On touching the body ſhe found that it was warm, and taking off the covering from his face, all were aſtoniſhed to find that the chief was alive. Seeing this, they took him back to his houſe, where he ſurvived for more than four months. This woman became pregnant at the age of 64, and was prematurely delivered, at the end of five months, of five infants, all alive.

Ruins of Copan.

Near here, on the road to the city of San Pedro, in the firſt town within the province of Honduras, called Copan, are certain ruins and veſtiges of a great population and of ſuperb edifices, of ſuch ſkill, that it appears they could never have been built by a people as rude as the natives of that province. They are found on the banks of a beautiful river, in an extenſive and well choſen plain, temperate in climate, fertile, and abounding in fiſh and game.

Among the ruins are trees which appear to have been planted by the hands of men, as well as

gradas. Sin lo dicho hay muchas cosas que demuestran haver havido alli gran poder i concurso de hombres, é pulicia, i mediana arte en la obra de aquellas figuras i edificios. He procurado con el cuidado posible saber por la memoria derivada de los antiguos, que gente vivió alli é que saben é oyeron de sus antepasados, i no he hallado libros de sus antigüedades, ni creo que en todo este districto hay mas que uno, que yo tengo; dicen que antiguamente havia venido alli i fecho aquellos edificios un gran señor de la provincia de Yucatan, i que al cabo de algunos años se bolvió á su tierra é lo dejó solo i despoblado, i esto parece que de las patrañas que cuentan es la mas cierta, porque por la memoria dicha parece que antiguamente gente de Yucatan conquistó i subjetó las provincias de Ayajal, Lacandon, Verapaz, i la tierra de Chiquimula, i esta de Copan, i ansi la lengua Apay que aqui hablan, corre i se entiende en Yucatan i las provincias dichas. I ansimesmo parece quel arte de los dichos edificios es como lo que hallaron en otras los Españoles que primeramente descubrieron la de Yucatan é Tabasco, donde huvo figuras de obispos, hombres armados, i cruzes, i pues en ninguna parte se ha hallado tal, si no es en los lugares dichos: parece que se puede creer que fueron de una nacion los que hicieron lo uno i lo otro.

De los lugares dichos me volvi á Guatemala, porque con indisposiciones de algunos del Audiencia fue necessario para el despacho de los negocios,

many other remarkable things. Before reaching them, we find remains of heavy walls, and a great eagle in ſtone, having on its breaſt a tablet a yard ſquare, covered with unknown characters.

Arriving at the ruins, we find another ſtone in the form of a giant, which the ancient Indians aver was the guardian of this ſanctuary. Entering the ruins we find a croſs of ſtone, three palms in height, with one of the arms broken off. (30) Further on we encounter ruined edifices, and among them a number of ſtones ſculptured with much ſkill; alſo a great ſtatue more than four yards in height, which reſembles a biſhop in his pontifical robes, with a well-wrought mitre on his head, and rings on his fingers. Near this, is a well built *plaza* or ſquare, with ſteps or grades, which, from deſcription, reſemble thoſe of the Coliſeum at Rome. In ſome places it has eighty ſteps, paved, and made in part at leaſt of fine ſtones, well-worked. In this ſquare are ſix great ſtatues; three repreſenting men with armor in moſaic, and garters around their legs. Their arms are loaded with ornaments. Two are of women, with long robes, and with head dreſſes in the Roman ſtyle. The remaining ſtatue is of a biſhop, who holds in his hands a packet reſembling a box or ſmall trunk. It ſeems that theſe ſtatues were idols, for in front of each of them is a large ſtone, in which is carved a ſmall reſervoir, with its groove, in which the blood was collected from the ſacrifices. We find alſo the

i anſi ſe mandó lo hicieſe, paſé por lugares bien frios é fragoſos donde ay los mayores i mas hermoſos pinos i robles, cedros, cipreſes, i otros muchos arboles que ay en todas eſtas provincias.

Eſtas ſon las coſas que en el diſcurſo de la viſita que hize por orden de V. M. me parecieron dignas de alguna conſideracion; no pongo entre ellas la orden i particularidades de ſu gentilidad por ſer muchas i requerir gran eſcriptura, aunque pudiera por tener hechas memoria de las mas dellas, ſiempre que V. M. me ocupáre en ſu ſervicio procuraré en lo general i en ſemejantes eſpecialidades de manera que ſe entienda, que a lo menos tengo buen deſeo.

Nueſtro Señor la C. i R. perſona de V. M. guarde muchos años con augmento de mayores eſtados i con felicimos ſuceſos! Deſta Vueſtra Ciudad de Guatemala, á 8 de Marzo de 1570 años. C. R. M. humilde i leal criado, que beſa las reales manos á V. M.

El Licenciado PALACIO.

FIN.

little altars on which the perfumes were burned before them. In the centre of the ſquare is a large baſin of ſtone, which appears to have ſerved for baptiſm; and in which alſo, ſacrifices may have been made in common. After paſſing this ſquare, we aſcend by a great number of ſteps to a high place, which appears to have been devoted to *mitotes* and other ceremonies; it ſeems to have been conſtructed with the greateſt care, for throughout we find the ſtones excellently well-worked. On one ſide of this ſtructure, is a tower or terrace, very high, and dominating the river which flows at its baſe. Here a large piece of the wall has fallen, expoſing the entrance of two caves or paſſages, extending under the ſtructure, very long and narrow, and well built. I was not able to diſcover for what they ſerved, or why they were conſtructed. There is here a grand ſtairway deſcending by a great number of ſteps, to the river. Beſides theſe things, there are many others which prove that here was formerly the ſeat of a great power, and a great population, civilized, and conſiderably advanced in the arts, as is ſhown in the various figures and buildings. I endeavored, with all poſſible care, to aſcertain from the Indians, through the traditions derived from the ancients, what people lived here, and what they knew or had heard from their anceſtors concerning them. But they have no books relating to their antiquities, nor do I believe that in all this diſtrict there is more than one,

which I poſſeſs. They ſay that in ancient times there came from Yucatan a great lord, who built theſe edifices, but at the end of ſome years returned to his native country, leaving them entirely deſerted. And this is what appears moſt likely, for tradition ſays that the people of Yucatan anciently conquered the provinces of Ayajal, Lacandon, Verapaz, Chiquimula and Copan; and it is certain that the *Apay* language which is ſpoken here, is current and underſtood in Yucatan and the aforeſaid provinces. ([31]) It appears alſo, that theſe edifices are like thoſe which the firſt Spaniards diſcovered in Yucatan and Tobaſco, where there were figures of biſhops, and of armed men, as well as of croſſes. And as ſuch things are found nowhere, except in the aforeſaid places, it may well be believed, that the builders of all were of the ſame origin. ([32])

From the aforeſaid places I returned to Guatemala, becauſe ſome of the members of the Audiencia had fallen ſick, and it was neceſſary for the deſpatch of buſineſs. In returning, I paſſed through places cold and rough, where there are the largeſt and moſt beautiful pines and oaks, cedars, cypreſſes, and many other varieties of trees, which are to be found in all theſe provinces.

Theſe are the moſt remarkable things which I diſcovered in the viſit which I made, under Your Majeſty's orders. I have not recounted all that I learned of the Indians during the time of their infidelity, becauſe it would make volumes; but I

can give what I have retained in my memory, if Your Majeſty thinks it uſeful, in ſuch a manner, at leaſt, as to prove my good will.

May Our Lord preſerve Your Royal and Catholic perſon for many years, with augmentation of dominion, and with happy deeds. From Your city of Guatemala, March 8th, 1576. Your Royal Catholic Majeſty's humble and loyal ſervant,

THE LICENCIATE PALACIO.

ILLUSTRATIVE NOTES.

Note 1, page 21.

FUENTES, and after him Juarros and the Bishop Pelaez, derive this name from the Tzendal words *Guhatez-mal-há* signifying *mountain which throws out water*, referring to the *Volcan de Agua* or Water Volcano, at the base of which stood the ancient city of Guatemala. That volcano, however, was called by the aborigines *Hunaphu*, mountain of verdure or of flowers, and does not seem to have been called *Volcan de Agua* until after the destruction of the old city of Guatemala, by a flood of water which poured down its sides on the night of the 11th September, 1541. Remesal, on the other hand, affirms that the word signifies, "lugar donde se echa la madera;" while Vasquez writes the original word *Quauhtemali*, "the same being a Mexican translation of the Kachiquel name *Iximche*, palo podrido." *Ixim* however, is the Kachiquel word for maize, and *che* means tree; the translation of Iximche, would therefore seem to be *maize-tree*, rather than *rotten-tree*. Juarros, however, suggests with great plausibility, that the name was derived from that of Juitemal, the first traditional king of Guatemala, and supports his opinion as follows: "It was a practice of "the native inhabitants to call kingdoms and towns by the names of the "monarchs or chiefs who governed them. Thus the natives of the "kingdom of Utlatlan were called Quichés from Nimaquiché, who led "them from Tula to that country; the Kachiquels from the kingdom of "Kachiquelch; the Zutugils from Zutugilch. In like manner, the "capital of Rabinaleb, Caçique of Vera Paz, was called Rabinal. And "even the Spaniards have followed the same nomenclature, by giving "the name Nicaragua to the territory of the Caçique Nicaragua, and "Nicoya to the possessions of the Caçique Nicoya."—*Historia del Reyno de Guatemala*, cap. xxxvi.

Note 2, page 21.

THIS language of Palacio bears a ſtrong likeneſs to that uſed by Cotton Mather, in writing of the Indians of New England:

" The natives of the country now poſſeſſed by the New Eng-
" landers, had been forlorn and wretched heathen ever ſince their firſt
" herding here; and though we know not *when* or *how* theſe Indians firſt
" became inhabitants of this mighty continent, yet we may gueſs that pro-
" bably the *devil* decoyed thoſe miſerable ſalvages hither, in hopes that the
" Goſpel of the Lord Jeſus Chriſt would never come here to deſtroy his
" abſolute empire over them. But our Eliot was in ſuch ill terms with the
" devil, as to alarm him with ſounding the ſilver trumpets of heaven in his
" territories, and make ſome noble and zealous attempts at ouſting him of
" his ancient poſſeſſions here. There were, I think, ſome twenty nations,
" if I may ſo call them, of Indians upon that ſpot of ground which fell
" under the influence of our then united colonies, and our Eliot was
" willing to reſcue as many of them as he could from that old uſurping
" *landlord* of America, who is by the wrath of God, the prince of this
" world.—*Magnalia Chriſti Americana*, b. iii; 1702."

Note 3, page 21.

IT would be intereſting to go into a critical analyſis of the liſt of languages given by Palacio, with a view of identifying the various dialects, and determining their relations. But this would involve a wide philological diſcuſſion, a compariſon of vocabularies, and an appeal to authorities quite beyond the ſcope of an illuſtrative note. And as the memoir of Palacio, after all, only relates to the diſtrict or provinces of Guazacapan and Izalco, and their immediate neighborhood, it will be enough to fix the relations of the dialects which were ſpoken in them, and which our authority declares were the *Popoluca*, *Pipil*, and *Chontal.*

The *Pipil*, it may be obſerved, was the prevailing language of the aborigines from the river Michatoyat to the river Lempa, including nearly the whole of the preſent republic of San Salvador, and was nothing more nor less than a dialect of the *Nahuatl* or *Mexican*. It is ſtill retained in moſt of the Indian towns, in the diſtrict referred to, but under the name of *Nahuatl.* The deſignation *Pipil* is now unknown, nor does it appear that it was ever adopted by the people themſelves. Etymologically it means childiſh, undeveloped, or provincial; and was probably applied by the Mexican auxiliaires in the armies of Alvarado and the con-

querors, as an expreſſion of contempt for a dialect which did not come up to their ſtandard of metropolitan purity.* Vocabularies which I procured from the Indians of this diſtrict, in 1853, ſhow very ſlight variations from the *Nahuatl* of the dictionaries—hardly greater than would be made by different perſons in writing down the ſame words, as they might be ſounded to them by the ſame individual. The principal variation is preciſely that which I have had occaſion to remark, in another connection, in the pronunciation of the *Nahuatls* of Nicaragua; viz, the general omiſſion or contraction of the well-known Mexican prefix and terminal *tl* or *tli*. Thus *tlativez*, to throw, becomes *tativez*, and *tlacatl*, man, becomes *tacat*. (See *States of Central America, etc.*, p. 338).

In the diſtrict proper of the Izalcos, the aborigines were undoubtedly wholly *Nahuatls;* but further to the weſtward, between the rivers Paza (the ancient Pazaca or Aguachapa), and Michatoyat, in the diſtrict called by Palacio *Guazacapan*, there were two languages ſpoken—the native or *Popoluca*, and the intruded or *Pipil*. This is, in fact, diſtinctly affirmed by Palacio in a ſubſequent paragraph. He ſays: "The Mex-"ican language is current among them, although their proper tongue is the "*Popoluca*." There is abundant evidence that the people of this diſtrict were not *Pipiles*, *Nahuatls* or *Mexicans*, nor yet of the ſame ſtock with the *Kachiquels* and their affiliated nations to the northward and weſtward. It was againſt them, and the people of Izalco and Cuſcatlan, that Alvarado was excited to make war by the Kachiquel kings, who furniſhed him with a large body of native auxiliaries for the purpoſe. He was three days in paſſing the belt of diſputed territory, depopulated and deſolate, which intervened between the Kachiquel territories and thoſe of the people of Guazacapan. His advance, ſays Juarros, was ſlow, becauſe "there was no intercourſe between the provinces, and roads were un-"known."

Herrara, in deſcribing Guazacapan, follows the ſtatements of Palacio. He ſays, "The natives of this province are ſubmiſſive, and ſpeak the "*Mexican* tongue, although they have another peculiar to themſelves. "When heathens they obſerved the rites of the *Chontals* of Honduras."—*Hiſt. de las Indias Occidentales*, dec. iv, lib. viii, cap. viii.

---

* Buſchmann conceives that the deſignation *Pipil* is a reduplication of the *Nahuatl* word *pilli*, having the double ſignificance of *child* and *nobleman*, like the German *jonker*. A late traveller in Nicaragua, Frœbel, thinks he has diſcovered the ſame word in *pipe*, a common term of endearment among the Indian and mixed population of that country.

We may fairly infer from this and other teſtimony, that the diſtrict was occupied by a people, probably of the ſame family with the nation or group of nations vaguely denominated *Chontals*, who had either been brought more or leſs under ſubjection to their *Nahuatl* neighbors, and been compelled to adopt their language, or who had gained a knowledge of it, and aſſimilated in other reſpects with them, from long contact and aſſociation.

The name of their peculiar language, according to the direct authority of Palacio, was *Popoluca;* and its relations, ſo far as we may infer from his teſtimony and that of Herrara, was with that of the people or peoples denominated *Chontals*. That it had ſome affinity with the language of the ſo-called *Chontals* of Honduras and Nicaragua, is ſupported by the circumſtance that a dialect called by that name was ſpoken in the towns Totogalpa, Telpaneca, Moſon:e, and Somoto-Grande, in the Department of Nueva Segoria, Nicaragua, as late as 1784-86. This department lies between the department of Chontales in Nicaragua, and that of Tegucigalpa in Honduras, and its phyſical and aboriginal affinities are the ſame. The concluſion is alſo ſupported by the fact that *Popolaca* and *Chontalli* are both pure *Nahuatl* or *Mexican* words, ſignifying ſtrangers, foreigners, and barbarians, or thoſe ſpeaking a barbarous language, which (as we ſhall ſoon ſee) accords with the uſe made of the term *Chontal*, as a general deſignation for all the ruder aboriginal nations of Central America. In Molina's Mexican Dictionary we have:

"*Popolaca*, barbero, hombre de otra nacion y lenguaje.

"*Popolaca*, que hablan lenguaje barbero. *Pret.* oni popolacac.

"*Chontalli*, eſtrangero, ó foraſtero."

The only inference that can be drawn from theſe data is, that the *Popoluca* was neither a dialect of the *Kachiquel* nor *Nahuatl*, but ſome form of the *Chontal*, uſing that term to deſignate the various dialects ſpoken by the "rude and brutiſh" Indian nations of the various provinces of Central America.

A language called the *Popoloca* was ſpoken by a portion of the people in the diſtrict around the ancient town of Tecamachalco, eighty or a hundred miles to the ſouth-eaſt of the city of Mexico. The Fray Franciſco de Toral, who afterwards became Biſhop of Yucatan, wrote a grammar of this language, which is characterized by Torquemada as "dificultoſiſima de aprender." The authorities always diſtinguiſh it as radically diſtinct from the Mexican; and, from all that can be gathered, the people who ſpoke it were an intruded family, of a warlike and obſtinate character. There is no reaſon for believing that their language had any relation with that ſpoken by the people of Guazacapan; although

it is probable that it received its name from the same cause, namely, its difficulty, and, to the Mexican ear, barbaric rudeness.*

I have grave doubts if the term *Chontal* was ever used to designate any particular language or dialect, and as a basis for an expression of my views on this point, I subjoin such allusions to the *Chontals* and the *Chontal* language as have fallen under my notice, in the early chronicles and in other authorities.

Torquemada alluding to the languages of Honduras, says: "There "are different languages, but the most general is that of the *Chontales*, "who extend into Nicaragua, called thus by the Spaniards, who mean "thereby to express rustics, or *Boçales*." †—*Monarchia Indiana, etc.*, vol. 1, p. 335.

Oviedo, enumerating the languages of Nicaragua, mentions three principal ones, of which the third was the *Chondal*. "These *Chondals*," he continues, "are the most clownish, living among the mountains or on "their slopes." In another place he adds: "The *Chondals differ* "*among themselves in language*, so that they cannot communicate one "with another; being separated in this respect as widely as the Bis-"cayans and Italians."

Palacio states that at Istepeque, in San Salvador, going southward, "The Indians commence to speak a new language, which they call "*Chontal*. They are very rude," etc. He again affirms, that in going from Chiquimula de la Sierra in Guatemala to Gracias á Dios in Honduras, "we find the *Chontal* Indians."

Herrara, probably following Oviedo, in enumerating the various nations of Nicaragua, mentions the *Chontals* as "a rude people of the "mountains." Copying Palacio, he speaks of the natives of Guazacapan, as "practicing the rites of the *Chontals* of Honduras, their neigh-"bors." He also states that in the Province of Tabasco there were spoken "three languages, the *Chontal* abounding in words and used by "a greater part (the masses) of the people, the *Zoque*," etc. In the same chapter, however, Herrara declares that Cortez, in taking care of the

---

* Dr. Carl Scherzer, and after him the Abbe Brasseur, speak of a dialect of the Kachiquel spoken in the mountains of Sacatapequez and near the town of Santa Maria in Guatemala, called *Pupuluka* by the first, and *Pa-puluka* by the latter. It would seem from the very imperfect data given by these authorities, that the designation was really *Puluka*, and quite local in its application. The Abbe Brasseur states that it comes from the name of a ruined town, near the present San Juan de Sacatapequez.

† The term *Boçales* here signifies simply persons speaking an unknown tongue, "muzzled," and is still applied in Cuba to freshly-imported negroes, incapable of understanding Spaniards, or being understood by them.

pacification of the various provinces on the North Sea, " no olvidodose " de la que llaman de Tabaſco, como tomó el nombre del cazique aſi " llamado, ſenor de Potonchan, que en lengua Caſtellana ſignifica *Chon-" tal*, como ſi ſe dixeſſe barbara, *porque lo miſmo es Chontal en lenguage Mexicana*."—*Decade*, iii, lib. vii, cap. iii.

In Molina's Mexican Dictionary (as I have already ſaid) the word *Chontalli* is defined as ſignifying " eſtrangero ó foraſtero."

It ſeems concluſive from the above references, that the term *Chontal* was applied, in various places, in the ſenſe of foreigners, " outſide barbarians," and ſavages, to the ruder Indian populations or tribes, and was never uſed ſpecifically to deſignate any particular family, and that, as applied to languages, it was uſed vaguely by the Mexicans, and after them by the Spaniards, to deſignate the languages of the peoples thus contemptuouſly characterized. The *Chontals* are always a rude, barbarous people, the loweſt in rank of the aboriginal families; and, according to Oviedo, " differing among themſelves *in language*, as widely as " the Baſques and Italians."

Hervas has fallen into ſome very grave errors in regard to a language which he calls *Chontal*, and which he imagines extended from Nicaragua to Tabaſco, and predominated in Guatemala. His deductions, however, as regards the diffuſion of the language, are excluſively founded on what is ſaid by Herrara, and above quoted; and his concluſion as to its having been the predominant language of Guatemala, reſults from a total miſapprehenſion of the ſame hiſtorian, and from a miſtake in underſtanding what Herrara ſays of the Province of Guazacapan ſpecially, as applying to Guatemala as a whole. (*Catalogue de las Lenguas Conocidas, etc.* vol. 1, p. 300). He underſtands Herrara to affirm, " que los " [Indios] de *Guatemala* tienen ſu lengua particular, y *obedecian á los " Chontales de Honduras*;" whereas Herrara, following Palacio, and in fact quoting from his Relacion, ſays this: " Son los Indios deſta Pro-" vincia [Guazacapan] humildes; corre entre ellos la lengua Mexicana, " aunque la tienen particular. Uſaban en ſu gentilidad de los ritos que " los *Chontales*, ſus vezinos; *obedecian mucho á ſus ſenores*, valia el que " mas podia, y el que era mas hombre de guerra," etc.

In diſcuſſing the ſubject, Hervas adds, that " en Nicaragua y Tabaſco " ſe habla la lengua *Chontal*, la qual ſeria la peculiar de los Guatemalaſes, " *porque eſtos eſtaban ſujetos á los Chontales de Tabaſco*," which is hiſtorically the reverſe of the fact; the Quichés, Zutugils and Kachiquels being in no degree dependent upon the Tabaſcans, but entirely independent of them, and much the moſt powerful.

I do not know on what authority it is ſtated that the *Chontal* language exiſted in Oaxaca. It might poſſibly be inferred from De

Souza's notice of the Fray Domingo Grijelmo, who, he ſays, went to Mexico in 1528, deſtined for the converſion "*de la ferociſma nacion* "*Chontal, cuyo lengua aprendió felizmente.*" He died in 1582, having written ſermons in the Zapoteca language. The Zapoteca was ſpoken in Oaxaca.

Note 4, page 23.

THE ancient province of Guazacapan, as defined by Palacio, is now entirely embraced in the Corregimiento of Guatemala, in the republic of the ſame name. The extent of coaſt between the Rio Michatoyat and the Rio Paz or Paza, the preſent boundary between Guatemala and San Salvador, is about fifty ſtatute miles. The ground near the ſea is low and full of creeks, correſponding with the deſcription in the text. This diſtrict was reduced by Alvarado, who here fought ſeveral ſevere battles with the various local chieftans; thoſe of the towns of Atiquipaque, Taxiſco and Guazacapan offering the moſt determined reſiſtance. Near the town of Comapa, which itſelf is near the boundary of San Salvador, are ſome conſiderable ruins, known as the ruins of *Cinaca-Mecallo*, for an account of which ſee my *States of Central America, etc.*, p. 341.

Note 5, page 29.

THE falls in the river Michatoyat, here alluded to, are ſaid by thoſe who have ſeen them, to be among the fineſt in the world. They occur near the village of San Pedro Martyr, in the department and republic of Guatemala. Mr. Stephens deſcribes them as "conſiſting of four ſtreams, ſeparated by granitic rocks, partly concealed "by buſhes, and precipitated from a height of about two hundred feet, "forming, with the wild ſcenery around, a ſtriking and romantic "view."—*Incidents of Travel in Central America*, vol. i, p. 292.

Note 6, page 31.

IN a previous note I have alluded to the change which this important paſſage has undergone in its tranſmiſſion through Herrara and Hervas, and how it has been underſtood by the latter to convey a ſenſe entirely different from that expreſſed in the original of Palacio. Another illuſtration of the neceſſity of following back the ſtream of American hiſtory to its ſource, is afforded in the ſame chapters of Herrara and Hervas, to which reference has already been made. Thus, what Palacio

ſays generally of the languages of the provinces of the old Kingdom of Guatemala as a whole, in the abridgment and paraphraſe of Herrara, is made to apply ſpecifically to the coaſt of the Pacific, between Guazacapan and the Rio Lempa. Hervas, following Herrara is thereby led quite aſtray in his philological deductions. Theſe corruptions of the original will beſt appear from the following compariſon:

Original of Palacio—1576.

"Eſtá dividida en 13 provincias principales, ſin otras mas menudas que en ellas ſe incluyen; ſon Chiapa, Soconuſco, etc.; i en cada una dellas ay i hablan los naturales diferentes lenguas, etc., que ſon: [Here follows an enumeration of languages, and Palacio reſumes;] De las quales [provincias] comenzé a viſitar de la de Guazacapan haſta el rio de Lempa, que corre 50 leguas al Eſte por la coſta del Sur, i á lo hancho haſta Chiquimula de la Sierra." etc.

Herrara's Paraphraſe—1601.

"Eſta dividida en 13 provincias principales, ſin otras menudas, que ſon Chiapa, Soconuſco, etc. * * * Todas los deſtas provincias hablan diferentes lenguas, començando de Guazacapan, haſta el rio de Lempa, que corre 50 leguas al Leſte, por la coſta del mar del Sur, y á lo ancho haſta Chiquimula de la Sierra," etc.—*Dec.* iv, *lib.* viii, *cap.* viii.

Note 7, page 33.

FUENTES, in his unpubliſhed Hiſtory of Guatemala, gives an account of ſome curious ceremonies practiced among the Kachiquels, Zutugils, Quichés, etc., on the occaſion of a childbirth. He ſays: "On the birth of a child they take an ear of maize, the kernels of "which are of bright and diverſe colors, and utter over it myſterious "and ſacred words, for the good of the infant. They cut the umbilical "cord with a new knife of flint, which has never been uſed for any "other purpoſe, and catch the blood on an ear of maize, which is then "ſhelled, planted, and carefully cultivated for the benefit of the child. "The produce is again planted for the child, which is ſupported from "the crop—a part, however, is given to the prieſt of the temple. Thus, "they ſay, they live, not by the ſweat of their brows, but from their "own blood. The knife uſed in the ceremony is regarded as a ſacred "thing, and is afterwards thrown in a river, to prevent future defile-"ment." He adds that in bringing up children "they faſten them to a "board, by means of ſtraps wound around their body all the way from "the feet to the ſhoulders, in conſequence of which all the Indians "have the backs of their heads ſmooth and flat."

Note 8, page 35.

THE so-called port of Istapa or Istapam, still answers to this description. It is simply a bad roadstead, without shelter, and only available, with difficulty, in the best of weather. In 1853 the government of Guatemala, formally abandoned Istapa, for a place twelve miles to the northward, called San José, which however seems to offer but a slight improvement on the former. Guatemala, unfortunately, has no natural port or harbor on the Pacific.

Note 9, page 37.

CACAO beans still serve for small change in the markets of Nicaragua, where five kernels have the value of about one cent of our currency. They have the same use in various parts of San Salvador and Guatemala. But the production of cacao, in the district around Sonsonate and Izalco, has greatly fallen off since Palacio wrote, and it is now quite a subordinate branch of industry. The natural adaptation of the country for its cultivation is, nevertheless, the same, and with peace and the introduction of capital, the ancient commerce in cacao may be revived, with increased amount and profit.

Note 10, page 39.

THE old friar, Thomas Gage, has left us a glowing account of the cacao, to which he confesses an extraordinary predilection. He says that " it contains the quality of the four elements, yet in the " common opinion of physicians, it is held to be cold and dry, *á praedo-* " *mino.* It is also in the substance that rules these two qualities, restringent " and obstructive, of the nature of the element of the earth. And as it is " thus a mixed and not a simple element, it hath parts correspondent to " the rest of the elements; and particularly it corresponds with the element " of air, that is heat and moisture, which are governed by unctious parts, " there being drawn out of the *cacao* much butter," etc., etc., through four pages. (*A New Survey of the West Indies, etc., English Ed. of* 1699, p. 239.) " The Peruvians," remarks Von Tschudi, " have some singu- " lar prejudices on the subject of eating and drinking. Every article of " food is, according to their notions, either heating *(caliente)*, or cooling " *(frio)*; and they believe that certain things are in opposition to each " other, or, as they phrase it, *se oponen*." (*Travels in Peru, American Ed.*, p. 105). The notion, it seems from the text, is as old as the days of Palacio.

Note 11, page 41.

THE city of La Trinidad de Sonſonate ſtill exiſts, and is one of the moſt thriving in the whole republic of San Salvador. It is ſituated, as deſcribed in the text, not far from the foot of the great volcano of Sta. Ana, formerly called Izalco—the latter name having lately been given to a new volcano or cone of eruption, which ſprung up in 1770, and has ſince reached an altitude of 4000 feet. The country around Sonſonate is fertile, thickly populated, and profuſely watered, in all reſpects anſwering the encomiums of Palacio. Juarros ſtates that the name of Sonſonate is a corruption of the Nahuatl or Mexican word *Cezontlatl*, ſignifying four hundred ſprings of water—a name not unwarranted by the multitude of ſprings and brooks which flow from the baſe of the volcano and the high lands near it, and give eternal freſhneſs and vigor to vegetation, and luxuriance and rich returns to the harveſt. Sonſonate is cluſtered round by Indian villages, of which Izalco is largeſt and moſt important, containing not leſs than 6000 inhabitants, moſtly Indians, who in part retain their native tongue and many of their original cuſtoms. No portion of the continent better deſerves the title of Garden of America, than the diſtrict of Sonſonate.

Acajutla, as deſcribed in the text, is a ſimple roadſtead, with no protection except what is afforded by a low ledge of rocks projecting into the ſea and called "Punta de los Remedios." At low water, and in calm weather, landing is eaſy; but at other times difficult, dangerous, and almoſt impoſſible. It is regarded as one of the moſt inſalubrious points, on the whole Pacific coaſt of Central America. Being however the only means of acceſs to a fertile and populous diſtrict, it muſt continue to be a reſort for commerce. Under the crown, it was one of the places of call for the Acapulco Galleons.

Note 12, page 43.

A recent traveller in Chiapas and Tabaſco, Mr. Morelet, ſays of the Rio San Pedro, a principal affluent of the great river Uſumaſinta: "Les eaux de cette rivière ſont douées à un haut degré de vertus pétrifiantes, et les écueils dont ſon cours eſt obſtrué, ſurtout aux environs de *Nojmactún*, n'ont pas d'autre origine que l'encroûtement et la ſolidification des troncs d'arbres qui y ſont tombés."—*Voyage dans l'Amerique Centrale*, vol. i, p. 307.

Note 13, page 49.

THE original is not very clear; but our author probably means to describe a spring, around which deposits and accretions have gradually formed a mass, like stone, with an opening in the centre, within which the water is constantly boiling, and from which smoke or steam constantly rises. Such springs, thus built in by their own deposits, are not uncommon. The one known as the Iodine Spring at Saratoga is of similar character. The other springs described by Palacio are now known by the name of ***Ausoles de Ahuacbapam***, and are among the most remarkable objects of curiosity in the country. They occupy a considerable tract of land, the largest being not less than a hundred yards in circumference. They emit a dense white steam, from a semi-fluid mass of mud and water, in a state of violent ebullition, which constantly throws off large bubbles, three or four feet in height. The water of the different springs varies in color, but otherwise their features are the same. The ground near them is hot, and soon becomes insupportable to the feet; and around all of them, the water has formed deposits of finest clays, of almost every variety of color, which, as suggested by Palacio, might be made useful in the arts. (*Gage's New View, etc.*, p. 415; *Montgomery's Narrative*, p. 115; *Stephens' Incidents of Travel in Central America*, vol. ii, p. 67). Not far from these springs, on a high ridge, is a remarkable volcanic lake called *Laguna Verde*, shut in by high precipitous walls of rock. It is only about three hundred feet broad, nearly circular, and of great depth. It has no outlet, but its waters are nevertheless sweet and potable. On the slope of the same ridge is a large intermittent spring vulgarly called *Agua Chsuca*, which flows freely from September to March, and is suspended for the remaining months of the year. Its water has a strongly fetid odor, and hence it derives its name.

Note 14, page 53.

THIS lake is distant two leagues to the southward of the present considerable town of *Cuatepeque*, from which it takes its name, *Laguna de Cuatepeque*. This name is derived from the Mexican *Coatl*, (in Pipil *coat* or *cuat*), serpent, and *tepec* or *tepeque*, mountain, i. e., Mountain of the Serpent. A considerable part of the limestone, for making the lime used in the town, is taken from the bottom of this lake, by divers. It is surrounded by abrupt walls of volcanic rocks, and seems to have been an ancient crater. The name of the town, as given in the text, *Coatan*, is compounded of *Coatl* as above, and *tlan*, place or locality of; i. e., Place of the Serpent.

Note 15, page 55.

THE ſtones called *chalchiuites* by the Mexicans (and written varioufly *chalchibetes*, *chalchibuis*, and *calchibuis*, by the chroniclers), were eſteemed of high value by all the Central American and Mexican nations. They were generally of green quartz, *jade*, or the ſtone known as *madre de Eſmeralda*, and were often elaborably carved with *relievo* figures of divinities, with hieroglyphics, etc. I have a number of theſe in my poſſeſſion, obtained from the ruins of Ocoſingo in Chiapas, not far from Palenque, which are real gems, far ſurpaſſing any works of aboriginal art which have fallen under my notice. The ſeated figure of *Cuculcan*, repreſented in bas relief, in one of the rooms of the palace at Palenque, and figured by Stephens, is reproduced in one of theſe *Chalchiuites*, in miniature. Another is a cylinder, reſembling the Aſſyrian or Babylonian cylinders, engraved with hieroglyphics on its outer ſurface. Among the preſents which Montezuma gave to Cortez for the King of Spain, were ſome of theſe ſtones. Bernal Diaz reports Montezuma as ſaying, in handing them over: "To this I will add a few *chalchibuis*, of ſuch "enormous value, that I would not conſent to give them to any one ſave "to ſuch a powerful Emperor as yours. Each of theſe ſtones is worth "two loads of gold." (*Lockhart's Tranſlation*, vol. i, p. 378). Diaz, in another place, ſpeaking of the ſkill of the ancient Mexicans in the arts, obſerves: "After theſe came the very ſkillful maſters in cutting and "poliſhing precious ſtones, and the *chalchibuis*, which reſemble the "emeralds." (*Ib.* vol. i, p. 233). And Fuentes, in his inedited hiſtory of Guatemala, deſcribes the Indians of Quiché as wearing "head-dreſſes "of rich feathers and brilliant ſtones, *chalchiguites*, which were large "and of great weight, under which they danced without wearying." The goddeſs of water, amongſt the Mexicans, bore the name of *Chalchiuilcuye*, the woman of the *Chalchiuites*, and the name of *Chalchiuhapan* was often applied to the city of Tlaxcalla, from a beautiful fountain of water found near it, "the color of which," according to Torquemada, "was between blue and green." Quetzalcoatl, the lawgiver, high-prieſt, and inſtructer of the Mexicans, was ſaid to have taught, amongſt other things, the art of working metals, and "en eſpecial el arte de labrar pie-"dras precioſas, que ſon *chalchiuites*, que ſon piedras verdes, que eſtima-"ban en mucho precio." (*Torquemada*, lib. vi, cap. xxiv). Quetzalcoatl, himſelf, according to certain traditions, was begotten by one of theſe ſtones, which the goddeſs Chimalma placed in her boſom. Torquemada ſtates alſo, that *chalchiuites* were offered to the goddeſs Matlalcueye, together with the plumes of the Quetzal. When a great dignitary died,

his corpse was richly decorated with gold, and plumes of feathers for burial, and " they put in his mouth a fine stone resembling emerald, " which they call *chalchihuitl*, and which they say, they place there as a " heart." (*Torquemada*, lib. xiii, cap. xlv).

Note 16, page 55.

THIS balsam is best known as "Balsam of Peru," from the circumstance that the early commercial regulations on the coast required it to be sent to Callao, before transmission to Spain, and the place of its origin being known to but few, it took the name of the country whence it was last received. The district in which it is obtained, known formerly as the Coast of Tonala, is now called Costa del Balsimo. It extends along the Pacific from the Port of La Libertad to that of Acajutla, a distance of fifteen leagues, and is exclusively inhabited by Indians, who still speak the Nahuatl or Pipil language, and retain their primitive habits and customs, little impaired. Their principal wealth is this balsam, of which they sell annually about 20,000 pounds. The trees yielding the balsam are very numerous in this privileged district, and seem to be limited to it; hardly a tree being found on other parts of the coast, which are seemingly identical in soil and climate. It is a large tree, with fine foliage, and its wood is of close grain, handsomely veined, resembling mahogany but of redder color. It takes a high polish and gives out a fragrant odor. The balsam is extracted by making incisions in the tree, in which are placed balls of cotton rags, in order to absorb the juice as it exudes. When these are saturated, they are replaced by others, and thrown into boiling water. The heat detaches the balsam, which being of less specific gravity floats on the surface of the water, whence it is carefully skimmed off, and gathered in calabashes or hollow sections of bamboo, for market. It has always been highly prized for medicinal purposes. In 1562 Pope Pius IV, and in 1571, Pius V, granted permission for its use in the consecration of the holy chrism. As stated in the text, it not only yields the black and white balsam, but also a nut, from which the " oil of balsam" is obtained, and flowers from which the " spirit of balsam" is distilled. The columns in the church of Guaymoco are now of this wood—perhaps they are the very ones seen by Palacio.

Note 17, page 55.

THIS is the ravine or *barranca* of Guaramal, a narrow cleft in the rocks, nearly a league in length, through which the road from Sonsonate to San Salvador still passes. It is traversed with difficulty,

the path lying, for a great part of the way, in the bed of the ſtream, over ſlippery rocks, and rough heaps of driftwood. The ſun never reaches ſome parts of the bottom of the barranca of Guaramal, and its cavernous aſpect is increaſed by the trees and buſhes which crown the rocks on either ſide, and in places form a complete arch of verdure. I obſerved amongſt theſe, when paſſing through the *barranca*, in 1853, a number of ſpecimens of the male or tree fern, of large ſize and great beauty. I believe it is found nowhere elſe in Central America.

Note 18, page 57.

MALPAYS or *malpais*, literally *bad country*, is a name applied throughout Central America to diſtricts overflowed by lava, or covered with volcanic ſtones and cinders. The lava-field croſſed by the high road between Maſaya and Managua in Nicaragua, is known as the *Malpais* of Nindiri.

Note 19, page 59.

HERRARA follows Palacio in his account of the ſtream referred to, in Chiapas. Juarros, who profeſſes to derive his information from an eye witneſs, affirms that "it is ſituated on the flank of a "mountain, half a league from the city of Ciudad Real, and is called "*Yeixhibuiat*, a Mexican word ſignifying 'three years water.' At the "expiration of the term of three years the fountain dries up, and the "waters burſt forth at a point five leagues diſtant, near the road of Teo-"piſca. The natives of that village give it the name of *Qbx-avilbu*, "which, in the Tzendal language, means the ſame with the Mexican "word. After flowing here for three years, the waters riſe again in their "former place."

Note 20, page 61.

THE city of San Salvador was founded in 1528 by George de Alvarado, brother of the conqueror, at a point called *las Bermudas*, in the vicinity of the preſent town of Suchitoto. About ten years after it was transferred to its preſent ſite. Under the crown it was the capital of the Province of San Salvador, and after the independence it became the capital of the State. For a ſhort time it was the ſeat of government of the Federal Republic of Central America. It was almoſt

entirely deſtroyed by an earthquake in April, 1854, when it was reſolved to change its ſite to the plain of Santa Tecla, about three leagues diſtant, and near the head of the barranca of Guaramal. The attempt was not ſucceſſful, and in January, 1859, it was again eſtabliſhed as the ſeat of government, on its ancient foundations. Beſides the earthquake mentioned by Palacio, the city ſuffered greatly by others which occurred ſubſequently, and of which thoſe of 1575, 1593, 1625, 1656, 1798, and 1839, are recorded as having been the moſt violent. The latter ſhattered the city, and led the people to think of abandoning it; but none of theſe convulſions ſeem to have been ſo ſevere as that of 1854. For a detailed account of the city and of this earthquake, ſee my "*States of Central America, etc.*," pp. 300–307.

Note 21, page 63.

THIS lake, named Ilopango (written anciently Gilopango) is about ten miles long, by perhaps five broad in its wideſt part, and is clearly of volcanic origin. It is ſurrounded on every ſide by high abrupt hills, compoſed of ſcoriæ, and volcanic ſtones. It receives no tributary ſtreams of importance, although it has a ſmall outlet, flowing through a deep, dark ravine, into the Rio Jiboa, near the baſe of the volcano of San Vicente. The water when taken up is remarkably pellucid, but it is not conſidered good for uſe. In calm weather it reflects the blue color of the ſky, but when its ſurface is ruffled by winds it aſſumes a green color, appropriately called *verde de perico*, parrot-green. It then emits a ſtrong and diſagreeable ſulphurous odor. At preſent, large quantities of the *mojarras*, referred to by Palacio, are caught by the Indians, and ſold in San Salvador, where they are greatly prized. The ſhores are divided out among the people of the ſurrounding villages, as their peculiar fiſhing grounds.

Note 22, page 63.

I have already given my reaſons for believing that the term *Chontal* was uſed not as a ſpecific but as a general deſignation, in the ſenſe of ſavage or barbarian, and applied by the Mexicans indiſcriminately to all frontier or uncivilized tribes with which they were acquainted, and often taken up and adopted by the Spaniards. There is no doubt of the fact that the ancient diſtrict of Chaparriſtique, now San Miguel, intervening between the river Lempa and the Bay of Fonſeca, was occupied by a tribe or number of tribes and families, differing in language cer-

tainly, and probably in origin and character from the Pipiles. Palacio ſtates that they ſpoke three languages, the *Taulepa*, *Poton*, and *Ulua*—the latter probably the ſame with the *Ulba*, which he alſo affirms was ſpoken in Honduras, where we can hardly fail to recognize it in the *Gaula* of Juarros, and *Woolwa* of modern times. It may be preſumed that the name is alſo perpetuated in that of the great river *Ulua*, the principal ſtream in Honduras, on the banks of which, according to the ancient chroniclers, lived the aboriginal family of the *Uluas*. The name *Taulepa* ſeems to be preſerved in that of the principal lake in Honduras, Lake *Taulebé* or Yojoa. The *Poton* is without doubt the ſame with the *Ponton* which Palacio mentions as having been ſpoken in Nicaragua. The teſtimony of the early writers indicates very clearly that the relations of the aborigines of the diſtrict of Chaparriſtique or San Miguel were with the Indians of Honduras. The fact that many names of places in that diſtrict are traceable etymologically to the Nahuad, may eaſily be overvalued. When Cortez undertook his expedition through Yucatan into Honduras, he was accompanied by ſeveral thouſand Mexican Indians, of whom many were left at the various ſettlements which he founded. The ſame was true of Alvarado. When he undertook the conqueſt of Guatemala, he had a very ſmall force of Spaniards, but a large body of Mexican auxiliaries. After the conqueſt was effected, lands were aſſigned to the latter in the vicinity of the conquered capitals, as well as in the neighborhood of the new eſtabliſhments that were founded by the Spaniards themſelves. It was thus that Almolonga and Mixco in the environs of the old city of Guatemala received their names; thoſe places having been aſſigned to a portion of the Mexicans in Alvarado's army. But this was not all. The Mexicans thus eſtabliſhed in the country often tranſlated the native names, in caſes where they characterized, as they generally did, ſome peculiarity of poſition or vicinage; and in ſome inſtances it is not to be doubted, they ſubſtituted names of their own for the native and, to their tongues, often unpronounceable names in uſe in the country. Thus the capital of the Zutugil kingdom was called *Atziquinixai* (home of the Eagle) by the Zutugils. The Mexicans, Pipils, or Nahuatls called it *Atitlan* (place by the water), it being ſituated on a lake. *Zetulul* they called *Zapotitlan*, and *Xelahuh*, *Quetzaltenango*. Examples of this kind might be greatly multiplied; but enough has been ſaid to ſhow that great caution is requiſite, eſpecially in Central America, in making deductions from the etymology of the names of places.

The language of the ancient inhabitants of the diſtrict of San Miguel, as far as can be aſcertained from the limited vocabularies of the Indians who ſtill ſubſiſt within its borders, was cloſely allied with the *Lenca*, as ſpoken by the Indians of Guajiquero, Similaton, etc., in Honduras, with

whom, as members of the ſame family, a conſiderable portion conſolidated themſelves, when they abandoned their ancient ſeats on the Pacific, in conſequence of the oppreſſions of the Spaniards and the incurſions of the buccaneers. It is therefore certain, both from direct and inductive evidence, that the aboriginal inhabitants of Chaparriſtique, at the time of the Conqueſt, were a diſtinct race from the Pipils of Cuſcatlan, and ſpoke a different language.

Note 23, page 65.

THE lake referred to in this paragraph is now known as lake Guija (written formerly *Guixar*), and is the largeſt in the republic of San Salvador, being not leſs than twenty leagues in circumference. It abounds in fiſh, the traffic in which is a ſource of conſiderable profit to the people living on its ſhores. According to tradition, the lake was formed by an eruption of the neighboring volcanos of San Diego and Maſatepeque. By theſe eruptions the channels of the rivers Oſtúa and Langue were blocked up, aud many ancient towns ſubmerged, the ruins of which the fiſhermen aver, they can ſtill diſcover at the bottom. On one of the iſlands in this lake, are the ruins of an aboriginal city, called *Zacualpa* or *Old Town*. There are alſo ruins of ancient edifices on the borders of the lake, and various treaſures have been taken from its depths; the laſt by an Indian fiſherman named Nicolas Santos, in 1848, who found in the crevices of a promontory of lava, left uncovered at low water, a large number of pieces of ſilver of round form, weighing altogether upwards of twenty-five pounds.

Note 24, page 65.

QUETZAL or *trogan reſplendens*, the imperial bird of the Quiché, Zutugil, and Kachiquel nations. It has a ſplendid plumage of a bright, metallic green color, and its tail feathers are often a yard in length. They were uſed by the civil and prieſtly dignitaries for purpoſes of ornament, and are repreſented as worn by the leading figures in all the ſculptures and paintings. The *Quetzal* is only found in the high and ſecluded mountains of Honduras, Guatemala, Chiapas, and perhaps in Oaxaca. Quetſaltenango, a department of Guatemala, has its deſignation from this bird; and the name combined with *coatl*, ſerpent, was that applied by the Mexicans to their great lawgiver, teacher, and demigod, *Quetzalcoatl*, who coincided with the *Cuculcan* of Chiapas and Yucatan.

Note 25, page 71.

CEREZADA, *contador* of the crown, who accompanied Gil Gonzales de Avila in his conqueſt of Nicaragua, gives a correſponding account of the rites and practices of the people of the Nahuatl ſtock, which were found around the lake of Nicaragua. Their mode of ſacrifice was the ſame; and they alſo punctured their bodies "rubbing the "blood from their wounds on the faces of their idols." They furthermore ſprinkled blood, drawn from the organs of generation, upon maize, which was afterwards diſtributed and eaten with great ſolemnity. This ſcenical rite, under one form or another, may be traced through the rituals of moſt of the ſemi-civilized nations of America, in ſtrict parallelism with certain Phallic rites of the Hindus, and of thoſe other numerous nations of the old world, devoted to a ſimilar primitive religion.

Cerezada ſtates that the temples of theſe Nicaraguans were built of timber and thatched, of large ſize, and containing many low, dark, inner chapels. Theſe, it ſeems, were ſurrounded by large courts, beyond which none but prieſts and cazique dared to paſs. Beſides theſe, there were what the Indians called *tezarits*, or "high places," conical or pyramidal in form, and aſcended by ſteps, on which the ſacrifices were made. They were flat at their ſummits, which varied in area, ſome being broad enough to give room for ten men. "In the middle of this ſpace," continues Cerezada, "ſtandeth a ſtone higher than the reſt, equalling a man's body "in length; and this accurſed ſtone is the altar of their miſerable ſacri-"fices. On the appointed day of ſacrifice, the prieſt, in full view of "all, from this eminent place, performeth the office of preacher, and "ſhaking a ſharp knife of ſtone which he holds in his hand, proclaims "that a ſacrifice is to be made, and alſo whether it be a priſoner, one "who is a ſlave, or one who has been reſerved from infancy for the "purpoſe. * * * Thoſe to be ſacrificed are ſtretched out flat on "the ſtone aforeſaid, and the prieſt cutting open the breaſt, plucks out "the heart, wherewith he anoints the mouths of the idols. The body "is then cut in pieces, and diſtributed among the prieſts, nobility and "people. But the head is hung as a trophy, upon the branches of cer-"tain ſmall trees, which are preſerved for that purpoſe near the place of "ſacrifice. The portions which are diſtributed they partly bury before "their doors, but the reſt they burn, leaving the aſhes in the field of "ſacrifice."

Juarros, quoting from the MS. Hiſtory of Guatemala, by the chronicler Fuentes, denies that human ſacrifices exiſted among the Pipils of Cuſcatlan. Fuentes baſes his ſtatement on a Pipil MS., to which he had

accefs, which gives, however, a very apocryphal not to fay abfurd account of the origin of the Pipils, and which affirms that the attempt to introduce human facrifices by the great cazique Cuauemichin, refulted in a general infurrection of his people, and his depofition and death. I, however, attach but little authority to the ftatements of this Pipil MS., and have no doubt of the exiftence of human facrifices among the people of Cufcatlan, as affirmed by Palacio, and after him by Herrara. The practice feems to have been univerfal among all nations of the Nahuatl or Mexican ftock, whether in Anahuac, Cufcatlan, or Nicaragua. Theirs was a bloody ritual, contrafting ftrongly with that of the various families of the great and more highly civilized Tzendal or Maya ftock.

Note 26, page 75.

THE name *Calpul* was applied by the Mexicans to what may be called the municipal edifices of their cities and villages. Thefe were placed around the public fquare of the various towns, frequently flanking or facing the principal temple or *cue*. Among the remains of ancient ftructures, on the fites of the abandoned aboriginal towns of Central America, we almoft always find a feries of truncated, terraced mounds of earth or ftone, difpofed in the form of a fquare, which to this day are called *calpules* by the common people. A fine group of thefe remains exifts in the immediate vicinity of the town of Sonfonate; another on the plain of Sta. Tecla or Nueva Salvador; and ftill another by the fide of the *camino real* defcending from the heights of Jiboa, near the city of San Vicente.

Note 27, page 79.

THE Fray Diego Duran, in his as yet unpublifhed "*Hiftoria Antigua de la Nueva Efpana, con Noticias de les Ritos y Coftumbres de los Indios, etc.*," written in 1585, gives very interefting accounts of the facrifices practiced by the Nahuatls of Mexico. He fays that one of the "greateft and moft folemn feafts was that of the idol called *Tezcatlipoca*, "which this fuperftitious people folemnized with many fingular rites and "facrifices, equalling thofe performed in honor of *Huitzlipochtli*. It was "called *Toxcatl*, a feaft relating to the number of their calendar which "was *Toxcatl;* but there was alfo another at this time in honor of "Tezcatlipoca—which idol, in the city of Mexico, was of a ftone of "very fhining black (obfidian, *itzli* or divine ftone) like jet—a ftone of "which they make arrows and knives. In fome of the cities the idol

" was composed of a tree carved in the figure of a man, all over black " from the face down, with the forehead, nose and mouth white, or of the " color of the Indians, clothed in gay dress, after the Indian fashion. In " its ears were rings of gold and silver, in the lower lip a bezoar stone, " and on its head plumes of red and green feathers. Back of the head " was the sign of smoke, indicating that he heard the prayers of sinners, " around the neck was a collar of gold so large as to cover the breast; " on the arms two bracelets of gold; at the navel a rich green stone; in " the left hand a fan of rich feathers, surrounding a circular plate of " gold, highly polished like a mirror, by which was meant that in this " was reflected all the doings of the world; it was called *Itlachia*, " Viewer. In the right hand some darts which signified that he punished " sins; for which reason he was held in great fear. At his feasts every " four years was granted remission of sins, on which occasion they slew " and ate an effigy of this idol. On the top of his feet he had 20 bells " of gold, and on the right foot the fore foot of a deer to signify his " lightness and agility in his works. It had also a cloak well worked, " black and white, with a fringe of red, black and white rosettes, and " adorned with feathers.

" The temple in which was this idol was very high and beautiful, " ascended by 80 steps, and at the top was a level space 12 or 14 feet " broad, and adjoining it a dark chamber, lined with rich cloths, of " various colors, with fringes of feathers, after the manner of ornamenting their temples, so that the chamber was obscure, and the idol dark " and mysterious. None except the priests dared enter here. In front " of the entrance to this chamber was an altar of the height of a man, " above which was placed a pedestal for the idol. The altar was like " those used by the Christians, and was covered with rich cloths. Above " the head of the idol was a costly canopy, adorned with feathers, gold " and precious stones.

" They celebrated the feast of this idol on the 19th of May, according " to our reckoning, and according to theirs it was the 4th feast of their " calendar and called Toxcatl. On the eve of this feast came the lord of " the temple, and put on new robes and ornaments, so as to resemble " the deity they were about to worship. Each idol had its peculiar " insignæ. When all was ready, they came to the temple called *Titlacauan*, and blew on a flute, first to the north, then to the east, south " and west—whereupon all knelt to the earth and taking up a little in their " fingers ate the same. When the thieves and other criminals heard the " flutes they were in great fear of vengeance from the gods, and sought " pardon. The soldiers and valiant men spent the day in listening to " the music, celebrating *Tezcatlipoca, Huitzlipochtli, Cihuacoatl, Quetzalcoatl* and the Sun, which are the principal gods whom they adore."

Note 28, page 81.

ACCORDING to Oviedo, the Fray Francifco de Bobadilla got together a number of leading perfons among the Nahuatls of Nicaragua, immediately after the conqueft, and queftioned them concerning their religion, their rites of burial, etc., thereby eliciting many curious and interefting facts, which illuftrate, in no fmall degree, the text of Palacio. They teftified that when their legitimate children died, they wrapped them in cotton cloth, and buried them before their doors. If a man died without children, his perfonal property was buried with him; if he had children, it was divided among them. On the death of a chief or cazique, "a portion of all his effects, cotton cloth, plumes, hunting "horns, gold and filver, etc., etc., was burned with his body, and, with "the afhes, gathered together and buried in an earthen vafe in the houfe "of the dead man." They believed that the *julio* or foul of the departed, if he had lived well, went on high, with the gods; if he had lived badly, it perifhed with his body and was no more. Fuentes ftates that in Guatemala, moft of the perfonal property of the dead was buried with them, and adds, that in fome parts they raifed over the corpfe "un cerillo, mas "ó menos alto, fegun la calidad del difunto; y efte fe fabricaba de piedra "y lodo, de que fe vean hoy infinitos por todas las llanuras de eftos "excelentes y fecundifimos valles, que llaman *cues*."

Note 29, page 83.

AMONG the Nahuatls of Nicaragua, according to Oviedo, marriage was a civil rite, performed by the cazique, and the ceremonies were much the fame as thofe practiced among the Mexicans. The matches were arranged by the parents of the parties; and as foon as the bargain was concluded, two fowls and a *rula* (a kind of houfe-dog) were killed, fome cacao prepared, and the friends and neighbors invited to the feaft. This finifhed, the cazique led the couple into a fmall houfe, devoted to that purpofe, in which a fire of refin was kindled, where, after giving them a lecture, he left them to themfelves. When the fire was burned out, the rite was complete. If it proved that the woman was not a virgin, fhe was fent back to her parents, and permanently difgraced, while the man was at liberty to marry again. The couple, after marriage, received from their parents a piece of land and certain fruit trees, which, if they died childlefs, reverted to their refpective families. But one wife was permitted to any man except the cazique, although concu-

binage was practiced by those who could afford it. Bigamy was punished by exile, and by confiscation of property for the benefit of the first wife or husband, who was then at liberty to marry again. This privilege was not however extended to women having children. Adultery on the part of the wife, subjected her to severe flogging, and to be sent back to her family; but she still retained her effects. It liberated the husband from his marital obligations; the woman, however, could not marry again. Relationship, beyond the first degree, was no bar to marriage. Marriages within families, on the contrary, were encouraged as "tightening the bonds of relationship." Incest was unknown; but the man who debauched the daughter of his master or cazique, was buried alive, with the partner of his guilt. The man who committed rape was seized, confined, and unless he could make reparation, by large presents, to the injured woman or her parents, became her or their slave. Sodomites were stoned to death. Prostitutes were tolerated, and the price of their favors limited to ten *amands* of cacao. They were accompanied by bullies, who however, did not share their gains. Establishments, or houses of prostitution, were kept publicly. On the occasion of a certain annual festival, it was permitted that all the women, of whatever condition, might abandon themselves to the arms of whomsoever they pleased. Rigid fidelity, however, was exacted at all other times.

Parents might traffic with the persons of their daughters, without subjecting themselves to punishment. Prostitution was sometimes resorted to by girls, whose parents were unable to provide for them a proper marriage portion. When one of these, having by this means, secured a competence, desired to withdraw from that mode of life, she procured a piece of ground whereon to build a house, and collecting her lovers, announced to them, that those desirous of having her for a wife, must unite and build a house, after the plan which she should furnish, and that when completed, she would select her husband from amongst them. The house being built and stocked, a feast was prepared, at the close of which the girl took the man of her choice by the arm and led him away, exulting to be preferred over his rivals. The rejected lovers, says the chronicler, "generally take it patiently, but occasionally one suspends "himself from a tree, in order that the devil may have his part in the "wedding, and is eaten for his pains."

Note 30, page 93.

ARCHÆOLOGISTS are aware that the early monkish writers placed great stress on the fact that crosses were discovered in various parts of America, at the time of the Conquest, whence

they deduced ſome very extraordinary concluſions. Don Carlos de Siguenza y Gongora ſpeaks of one taken from the cave of Mixteca-baxa, and venerated in his day, in the convent church of Tonola, dedicated to St. Dominic. This croſs, he avers, was "diſcovered by the muſic of "angels being heard in ſaid cave, on every vigil of the apoſtle St. "Thomas," who, according to this pious hypotheſis, introduced Chriſtianity into America, immediately after the era of Chriſt. Gomara, Bernal Diaz, and others mention croſſes in Yucatan, and Boturini teſtifies to having frequently met with them in the paintings. His error however, conſiſts in miſtaking the ſymbolical *Tonacaquahuitl*, or Tree of Life, for a croſs. This is not the place to attempt an explanation of the ideas connected with this ſymbol, which has lately been taken as one of the evidences of Phœnician eſtabliſhments in America! It may be obſerved however that the ſacred tree was variouſly repreſented, always of courſe in a conventional ſpirit. In ſome caſes its branches took the form of a croſs, ſurmounted by a bird, and ſurrounded by various ſymbols. This form was retained in a few of the monuments, as well as in the paintings, as will be ſeen by reference to the principal tablet diſcovered by Mr. Stephens at Palenque, in what he denominates Caſa No. 2. I alſo found monolithic figures, ſculptured in the form of croſſes, among the ruins in the iſland of Zapatero, in Lake Nicaragua. (*Nicaragua, its People, Scenery, Monuments, etc.*, vol. ii, pp. 58-62).

Note 31, page 96.

THIS paragraph is omitted in Terneaux Compan's tranſlation. Mr. Stephens obtained a brief vocabulary at Zacapa, thirty miles to the northweſt of Copan, which he communicated to Mr. Gallatin, by whom it was publiſhed (*Trans. Am. Ethnological Soc.*, vol. i, p. 9). Of this dialect Mr. Gallatin obſerves (*Ib.*, p. 6) that "It appears to be "the general language of the department of Chiquimula, and extends "eaſterly, as far at leaſt as the ſite of the ancient Copan." The Chorti however, as given in the vocabulary of Stephens, is only a dialect of the ſame mother tongue, of which the Maya, Kachiquel, etc., are varieties. This is perfectly conſiſtent with the hypotheſis that it is the ſame with that denominated by Palacio the Apay, and which he affirms coincided in all eſſential reſpects with the languages current in Yucatan, and in the provinces of Vera Paz and Chiquimula.

Note 32, page 96.

TO the teſtimony of Cortez, Bernal Diaz, Gomara, and Torquemada, as to the extent and ſplendor of the temples and public edifices of Mexico and Yucatan, I may add that of Las Caſas in regard to thoſe of Central America, conſtituting part of Chapter lii of his *Hiſtoria Apologetica*, as yet unpubliſhed. The original MS. is not very clear, and there are evident miſtakes by the copyiſt, but I prefer to give the text *verbatim et literatim*, without any attempt at emendation or improvement.

"En el Reyno de Guatemala, en la parte que va por la Sierras, eſtaban "ciudades de caba muy grandes, como era lo que ſe llamaba Guatemala, "y otra que era como la cabeza del Reyno, llamada Utlatan, con mara-"villoſos edificios de cal y canto, de los cuales yo ví muchos; y otros "pueblos ſin numero de aquellas ſierras.

"Por la parte de los llanos de la coſta de la Mar del Sur, toda tierra "felicíſima, cuando al principio entraron en aquella tierra los Eſpagñoles, "eran tantos y tan grandes los pueblos y lugares y de tan immenſas "gentes poblados, que los que iban delante volvian muchas veces atras al "capitan, pidiendole albricias que habian hallado otra ciudad como la de "Mexico; y eſto cuaſi á cada paſo, como los veian tan grandes.

"El Reyno de Yucatan que dura mas que dos cientas y cincuenta "leguas ſus contornos, los edificios admirables que tenia y hoy eſtan harto "claros no parece que ſon menos dignos de admiracion, que las pira-"midés. Habia los tantos y tales y tan grandes, y en ellos coſas ſeñaladas "y de notar que parece haber ſido impoſible por hombres edificarlos.

"Entre otras coſas memoraliſimas que alli habia eran que como toda "aquella provincia ô reyno ſea todo llano, y el ſuelo cubierto de las laxas "ó peñas llanas de que arriba, en el Cap. 30, digimos ſer la provincia "de Hyguey de eſta iſla como naturalmente ſolada y toda de arboladas "cubierta, eſtaban hechos unos como grandes montes ó ſierras de tierra, "y ſobre ellos edificios de piedra y canteria, labrados y fundados ſobre "fortiſimos y eſtraños cimientos ſu cima de lo alto, de los cuales habia "hechos de bóveda otros mas artificioſos y fuertes y pulidos, que ſolo en "un cuarto de cuartro pueden caber cien hombres bien apoſentados.

"Tienen algunos de circuito media legua y no mucho menos, y vanſe "hácia lo alto enſangoſtado cuaſi como las pyrámides. Parece que "millares de gente no podian haberlos edificado en cicuenta años. "Tienen eſculpidas en las piedras muchas imágenes y antiguallas; y aun "dieeſe que parecen tener letreros que digan algo de ciertos caraćteres. "Preſúmeſe haber ſido ſepulturas de Reyes y Señores grandes.

"La Provincia que llamamos de Honduras tenia pueblos innumerables y

" una vega de treinta leguas y mas, toda muy poblada. La provincia de " Naco y de Zula, la ciudad de Naco, que tenia ſobre dos cientos mil " animas, y muchos edificios de piedra, en eſpecial los templos en que " adoraban.

" La Regia y felicíſima provincia de Nicaragua? quien numerará ſus " poblaciones tantas y tan grandes? Y como ſea tan anciana y de fructas " ſuaviſimas tan abundante, primero ponian los arboles y frutales que los " pueblos edificaſen.

" La de Nicoya que es en el miſmo Reyno de Nicaragua, hacia el " Golfo que entra en la tierra bien doce leguas, lleno de iſlas pobladas, " toda á la Mar del Sur; ſus pueblos y numeroſidad de vecinos eran " grandes, pueſto que las caſas no eran de piedra ſino de madera muy " bien hechas y cubiertas de paja. Comunmente donde la tierra es " fria todas las caſas de los pueblos ſon de madera y paja, y en muchas " partes las cubren de hojas de palmas por que las hay tan anchas como " una rodela y cuaſi en partes como una adarga. Siempre los templos " edificaba de piedra ó de adobes por lo alto cubiertos de paja, pueſto " que no en todos, pero en muchas partes."

Fuentes ſpeaks of the numerous large towns and cities found in Guatemala as proof that its aboriginal ſovereignties were ſcarcely leſs powerful than thoſe of Guatemala and Peru. He mentions particularly the public buildings of Gueguetenango, Chialchitan, and others found in the department of Vera Paz and " la fabrica marabilloſa y ſubterranea del pueblo " de Puchuta que ſiendo de firmiſima y ſolida argama ſe camina y corre " por lo interior de la tierra por diſtancia prolongada de nueve leguas, " haſta el pueblo de Tecpan Goatemala, que es argumento y prueba del " ſoberano poder de aquellos reyes, y numeroſidad ſin calculo de los " vaſallos que los obedecian." He ſpeaks alſo of the great fortreſs of Parraſquin, " la memorable y prodigiſa fortaliza," which is ſeen deſcending from Totonicapan, on the South coaſt. Looking at all things, he ſays, " me hace creer que aun no podre comprender para eſcribir todo lo " que hay de marabillas ſingulares en eſtas nuevas y apreciables pro- " vincias."

To the ſame effect is the teſtimony of Dr. Alonzo de Zurita, Auditor of Mexico, who wrote before Palacio, in 1554. He viſited Utlatan and Guatemala, and has left us ſome intereſting particulars concerning thoſe regions in a MS. relation which formerly exiſted in the library of the college of San Pedro y San Pablo in Mexico, where it was ſeen and copied by Boturini:

" En Utlatan habia muchos y muy grandes *cues* ó templos de ſus " Idolos, de marvilloſos edificios, y yo vi algunos aunque muy arruina- " dos; y alli tenian cues otros pueblos comarcanos, y el mas principal

" de eſtos el de un pueblo que llaman Chiquimula, y tenian á eſte pueblo " de Utlatan como ſantuario, y á eſta cauſa habia en el tantos y tan " principales cues. El Señor de Chiquimula ſolia tener mucha gente y " pueblos, y quando alli eſtube lo vi muy pobre y miſerable."

INDEX.

SPANISH ERRATA.

Page 18, line 1, for *variadades*, read *varidades*.
" 22, " 9, for *mucho*, read *muchos*.
" " " 16, a comma after *han meneſter*.
" " " 18, for *gaſta*, read *gaſtan*.
" " " 26, for *alliende*, read *allende*.
" 24, " 5, for *admira, aunque*, read *admira aun, que*, etc.
" 26, " 28, for *ſeparan*, read *ſe páran*.
" 28, " 7, for *el*, read *ella*,
" " " 9, for *ſe*, read *ſi*.
" " " 20, for *la*, read *lo*.
" " " 23, for *vuelvan* read *vuelven*.
" " " 24, for *ſeparan*, read *ſe páran*.
" 30, " 1, for *heran*, read *i heran*.
" " " 2, after *poderoſos*, put ſemicolon.
" " " 3, ſuppreſs ſecond *mas*.
" 32, " 11, comma after *ſerbido*, and for *ſepaſe*, read *ſe paſe*.
" " " 18, comma after *dicho*.
" " " 25, for *mudarſe*, read *mudaſſe*.
" 34, " 4, for *remarſo*, read *remanſo*.
" " " 5, for *entra*, read *entrado*.
" " " 10, comma after *hacer*.
" " " 11, dele comma after *corriente*.
" " " 14, inſert *es* after *Que*.
" " " 20, for *comunamente*, read *comunmente*.
" " " 25, for *todas*, read *todos*.
" 36, " 27, for *quartro*, read *quatro*.
" " " 29, for *contó*, read *conté*.
" 38, " 15, for *ha*, read *han*.
" " " 25, for *poſicion, ſuſtentarſe*, read *poſicion ; ſuſtentanſe*, etc.
" 40, " 1, for *falto de otro tal, e toda eſta comarca*, read *falta de otro tal en toda eſta comarca ;* etc:
" " " 9, for *Eſpedido*, read *Eſpelido*.
" 42, " 4, for *ifertilidad*, read *i fertilidad*.
" " " 20, for *engañandas*, read *engañadas*.
" 44, " 4, for *mamada averigue*, read *mamaba, averigue*, etc.
" " " 9, for *quiſe*, read *que ſe*.

Page 44, line 13, put comma after *miſericordia*.
" 46, " 1, ſemicolon after *medico*.
" " " 3, colon after *mucho*.
" " " 7, for *bacia* read *baria*.
" " " 20, put *que* after *humo*.
" 48, " 8, for *ſale*, read *ſabe*.
" 50, " 3, for *dicho*, read *dicha*.
" " " 5, for *is*, read *es*.
" 52, " 10, for *Con*, read *En*.
" 54, " 20, for *auſi*, read *anſi*.
" " " 22, dele comma after *fuego*.
" " " 23, put ſemicolon after *volcan*.
" " " 24, for *que manda*, read *quemada*.
" 56, " 10, for *otra*, read *otro*.
" 58, " 16, 17 ; put period after *Eſpantada*, and read *En los arrabales de la Cuidad, ſalen tres hojos*, etc.
" 60, " 1, for *que*, read *de*.
" " " 10, for *ella*, read *ellos*.
" " " 22, for *tienan*, read *tienen*.
" 64, " 8, for *colorados*, read *coloradas*.
" " " 18, for *habia*, read *habian*.
" 68, " 7, for *hechá*, read *hechas á*.
" " " 21, for *cerra*, read *cerraban*.
" 70, " 1, for *por*, read *para*.
" 72, " 2, colon after *manos*.
" " " 4, for *mana*, read *mano*.
" 74, " 1, after *ſacerdotes*, put *ſe*.
" " " 29, for *chamuſcado*, read *chamuſcada*.
" " " 16, ſemicolon after *tizne*, and dele comma after *ſignificara*.
" " " 19, for *cortarban*, read *cortaban*.
" 78, " 29, dele ſemicolon after *rio*. and inſert comma after *ambos*.
" 84, " 2, after *gentilidades*, inſert *que*.
" " " 22, for *dellos*, read *dellas*.
" 38, " 1, for *trae*, read *traen*.
" " " 6, for 1764, read 1564.
" 88, " 28, for *mitro*, read *mitra*.
" 90, " 1, for *grados*, read *gradas*.
" " " 5, for *eſta*, read *eſtan*.

ENGLISH ERRATA.

Page 10, line 8 from top, for *Olofingo*, read *Ocofingo*.
" 51, line 3 from bottom, for *venemous*, read *vonomous*.
" 100, line 1 from bottom, for *auxiliaires*, read *auxillaries*.
" 102, line 15 from top, for *Nueva Segoria*, read *Nueva Segovia*.
" " lines 24 and 25 from top, for *barbero*, read *barbaro*.

www.ingramcontent.com/pod-product-compliance
Lightning Source LLC
Chambersburg PA
CBHW020747020726
47495CB00008B/2346

9783337176396